# A HISTORY OF WHITEFIELD PUBS

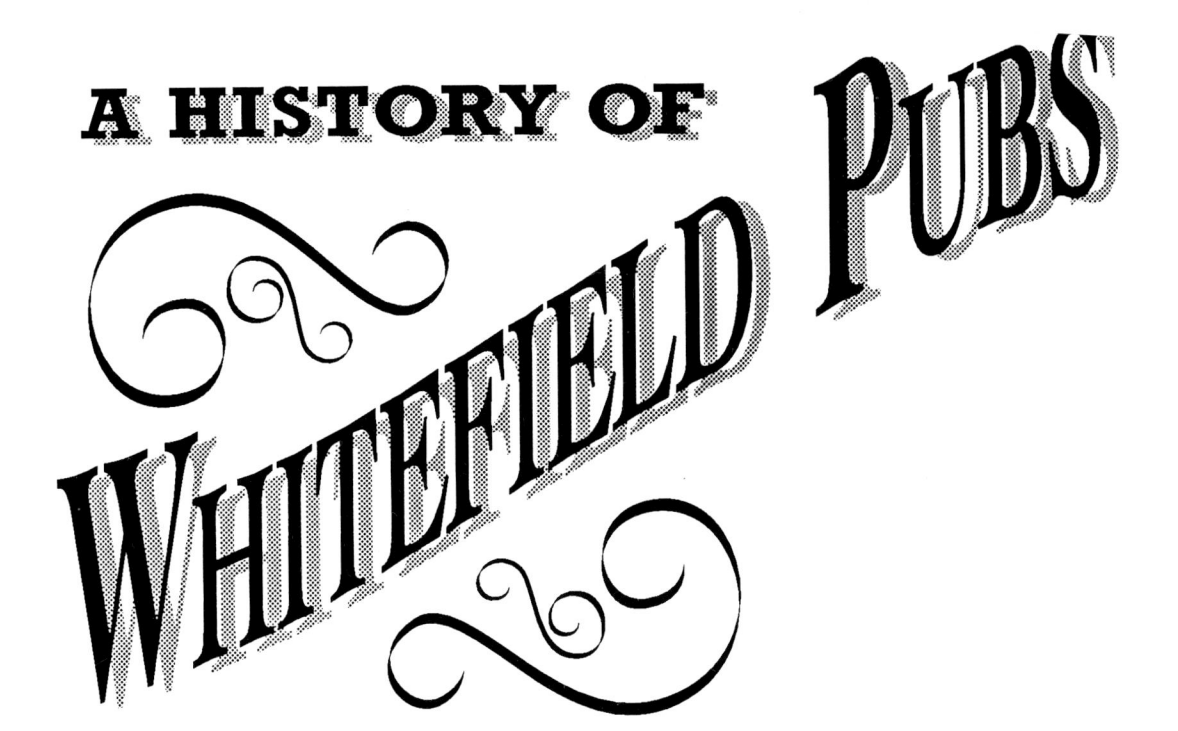

'There is nothing which has
yet been contrived by man by
which so much happiness is
produced as by a good
Tavern or Inn.'

Dr Samuel Johnson 1709-84

**Researched and written by Glenn Worth**

**Published by Kenyon Publishing, 1 Kenyon Lane, Prestwich, Manchester M25 1HY**

Typesetting and editing by Roger Pearson MA

Cover design by Robert Long Tel 061 643 6474

Printed in Great Britain by Printcentre, Crown House, Trafford Park Road, Trafford Park, Manchester M17 1HG

*A History of Whitefield Pubs*

# Links with the Past

Whitefield, when compared with many other places in Lancashire, may be said to lack a definite history and yet there is a distinct note of antiquity about the place.

For the township of Pilkington, of which Whitefield was once a constituent part, derived its name from the historic family of that name, a name which has given many soldiers and Ecclesiastics to the roll of fame throughout our English history. There is on record the fact that a Leonard de Pilkington fought at the battle of Hastings in 1066 over nine hundred years ago.

The name 'Pilkington' can be readily explained by taking the meanings of its syllables. The last part 'ton' signifies a place of dwelling, not necessarily a house but more a village or town; the 'ing' which is short for 'ingar' is used in the sense of 'offspring of' or more modernly 'belonging to'. The Pilk part of the word is the name of the family itself; the full name taken together - the town of the family of Pilk.

With the Norman conquest came these Pilkingtons and here they remained for hundreds of years. Many English Kings held them, each in his day, in high esteem and as was the experience of most knightly families, they were, at different times in their history, exalted and degraded, honoured and despised in high quarters of Church and State.

The crest of the Pilkington family was a Mower with his scythe and the motto '**Now thus, Now thus**'. Differing accounts for the reason for this are given, but according to Fuller's 'Worthies of England' the chief of the family, being sought after at the time of the Norman conquest, was forced to disguise himself as a mower in a field and he afterwards used that device as a crest for his helmet.

The words 'Now thus, Now thus' were traditionally said to express the motion of the scythe in mowing. It is just possible that the words were the chorus or refrain of an old scythe song which set out to imitate the rhythmical rushing sound of the scythe in mowing through the grass. Another explanation was that this disguised member of the family held the scythe the wrong way and when his attention was drawn to the fact, he immediately exclaimed '*Now thus, Now thus*' and reversed the scythe as he repeated the words.

**The Pilkington Coat of Arms**

The crest and motto combined show clever handling of the facts of those who devised the coat of arms. They were able to convey historical meaning in a very small compass. The figure of the mower, being half in white and half in black, half in rustic costume and half in armour, depicts disguise as well as a change of fortune. The bearer of this coat of arms was once 'Now thus' as a rustic and 'Now thus' as a knight. Many inn signs depict some historical event in the same way and survive to this day.

One Pilkington left Stand in 1108 and went on the first crusade to the Holy land, returning two years later. Yet another, Roger Pilkington, was an important knight of the shire and he lived in the fourteenth century when the serfs of Lancashire were slowly but surely making their efforts for greater freedom.

The wars of the Roses had a definite bearing on the history of the Pilkington family and Sir Thomas was a faithful adherent of the Yorkist cause and he mustered his followers and fought at Bosworth Field in 1485.

It was in this battle that the Earl of Derby with his following stood aloof at the beginning of the battle and at a critical period marched against Richard III. Bringing about his rout, complete downfall and death, when the successful King Henry VII was firmly seated on the throne Sir Thomas Pilkington, the lord of the manor, was attainted (charged with treason) and the family fell from its high estate. The manors of Pilkington and Bury were bestowed and granted to Thomas, first Earl of Derby. He played a conspicuous part at the battle of Bosworth Field in 1485, although then he was a Stanley. Considered to be a loyal follower of Richard, his desertion to the side of Henry Tudor, after the battle had been in progress some time, brought about the end of the Plantagenet Kings and the commencement of the Tudor dynasty. His wife, Margaret Beaufort was actually the new King's mother and it was he who actually crowned Henry on the battlefield.

In the period of the Jacobite rebellions and general unrest the people of Whitefield were divided in their allegiance either to the Stuarts or the Hanoverians. The majority of the adherents to each of the two parties lived on opposite sides of the main road and much trouble often resulted.

Until the nineteenth century Whitefield existed only as a part of the manor of Pilkington, which covered not only Whitefield, but also the districts of Outwood, Stand, Ringley, Unsworth, Hollins and Besses o'th' Barn.

Over the centuries hamlets grew up in the Lily Hill district, at Besses o'th' Barn, at Park Lane, at Moss Lane and at Stand. These hamlets, together with Stand Lane (now part of Radcliffe) were united as the Township of Whitefield in 1866.

How the hamlet came by the name Whitefield is uncertain. The possible origin of the name goes back to the time when the Flemings were welcomed to our shores to introduce weaving. The first settlement was in Suffolk, then one followed in the East Lancashire valley south of Rossendale Forest (Whitefield was on the southern edge of the forest) where there were '*fields*' or open patches of ground where woven materials could be bleached in the open air and as these pieces lay about on the ground the appearance of a '*White field*' was a natural one.

As it is also thought the name Whitefield might have existed before the Flemings settled here, it may be derived from a field of white flowers, hence the name Lily Hill street; or it could also be a derivation of 'Wheatfield'.

### Origin of 'Stand'

*The derivation of the word 'Stand' stems from the fact that hundreds of years ago east Lancashire was very wooded and there was much hunting. Stand Hall had been the Pilkington family seat for centuries, and this was be the gathering place for the hunting gentry.*

*The name 'Stand' derives from a hunting stand, a risen platform from which the countryside could be scanned for game.*

# Contents

| | |
|---|---|
| Links with the Past | 2 |
| Acknowledgements | 4 |
| Introduction | 5 |
|    The Earliest Surviving Alehouse Recognizance for Pilkington | 6 |
| Albert Inn | 8 |
| Besses o'th' Barn Inn | 10 |
| The Bull's Head | 14 |
| Black Horse Inn incorporating the Victoria Inn | 16 |
| The Bay Horse | 18 |
| Public House Terms | 22 |
| Bay Horse | 24 |
| Brown Mare | 28 |
| Beehive Inn | 29 |
| Coach & Horses and Bentley Brewery | 34 |
| Church Inn | 39 |
| Cross Keys | 43 |
| Corner Cupboard | 47 |
| The Dragon | 49 |
| Derby Hotel | 50 |
| Eagle and Child | 53 |
| Whitefield Brewery | 55 |
| Elizabethan | 59 |
| The Frigate | 59 |
| Foresters | 60 |
| Goats Gate Inn | 62 |
| Junction Hotel | 67 |
| Royalty and Beer | 72 |
|   Other Interesting Facts | 72 |
| Lord Clive | 73 |
| Masons Arms | 74 |
| New Grove Inn | 78 |
| Parkfield Inn | 80 |
| Queen Anne | 82 |
| Robin Hood | 84 |
| Red King (and William IV) | 87 |
| Rose and Crown | 89 |
| Seven Stars | 91 |
| Travellers Inn | 92 |
| Wheatsheaf Hotel | 94 |
| Woodman Inn | 97 |
| Welcome Inn | 98 |
| The Origin of Beer Engines | 102 |
| Epilogue | 104 |
|   Interesting Facts | 104 |
|   A Celebration in Verse | 105 |
|   And a Few Tales | 105 |
|   Landlord! Beerhouse! Pub! | 106 |

# Acknowledgements

The Author would like to express his sincere gratitude to all those listed below for helping in whatever way they could to make this **pub**lication possible.

Special thanks to the following:

Ken Miller, who in his retirement mastered the intricacies of his new word processor and copied out all my handwritten text into a format which enabled me to calculate just what would fit into these pages and what wouldn't!

David Rowlinson, Author of 'History of Prestwich Pubs' for donating research material, gathered earlier

Sue and Neil Richardson for their much appreciated contribution.

Eric Heath who has copied and processed the majority of the photographs and gone enthusiastically on many an 'assignment' with his cameras and tripod, for many of the present day photographs.

Editor's thanks to Julia and Jessica Pearson for everything.

## Individuals

(All of whom kindly loaned items for copying)

Lily Marshall
May Barker
Louie Schofield
David and Joan Hamer
Frank Williams (Unsworth)
Harry Fletcher
Fred Butterworth
Joe Pearson
Hartley Kirby
Brian Derman (Ex Junction Inn)
Annie Aldersey (Ex Goats Gate)
Lynn Hesketh
John Hannan (Beehive)
Rick Hartree
Ronnie and John Bentley
Charles (Bob) Braid
Ken Shenwell

## Computer Services

Patricia Taylor (word processing)
(Big John) Smith BA (Hons)

## Photography

Glenn Worth: Present day photographs
Eric James: Photograph restoration technician
Roger Pearson, MA: Computer extraction of stills from film

## Libraries

Whitefield: David Galloway
Prestwich: Harry Wilkinson
Unsworth: All staff
Bury (reference): All staff
Central Library: Ms De Motte, Assistant Librarian, local history library

## Archives

Bury Archives: Kevin J Mulley
Greater Manchester Archives, Marshall Street: All staff
Lancashire Records Office, Preston: K Hall, BA DIP Archive Admin County Archivist
Bury Magistrates Court (Licensing Section): Chris Reid, Miss Fletcher

## Newspapers

Manchester Evening News
Bury Times
Prestwich and Whitefield Guide
Radcliffe Times
The Advertiser
Evening Chronicle (1952)
Manchester Guardian (1906), (1857)
Manchester Magazine 1748-1749

## Granada Television

Dominique Faure, Publishing co-ordinator

## Breweries

**Whitbread**:
Roger Wadsworth, FRICS, Chief Surveyor (1981)
M F Mallinson, Area Surveyor (1981)
Caroline M Normanton Bsc (Hons), Assistant Estate Manager (1991)
**Greenhalls**:
Mrs A Riley, Property records administrator (1991)
**Daniel Thwaites**:
J Wilcock Group Property Manager (1992)
**Frederic Robinsons**

## Bibliography

Thomas Holt: Pilkington Park, 1962

BT Barton: History of the Borough of Bury and Neighbourhood 1892

Bertram F Buttery (Ed): Whitefield Festival Souvenir Handbook 1951

Joseph N Hampson: History of Besses o'th' Barn Band 1892

Neil Richardson: A History of Joseph Holt 1984

WGS Hyde: The Manchester, Bury, Rochdale Tramway 1989

Alan Gall: Manchester Breweries of Times Gone By

## Pub Paintings and Drawings

Paintings: Ken Greenhalgh
Drawings: Gilda Dickinson

## Pubs and People

It would be totally insensitive to end these acknowledgements without mentioning the pubs themselves, the licensees and their customers in our present time and those in days long distance gone, for without what is happening and has happened, there would be no pub history to write about

### Dedication

*Finally, Ann-Marie whose enduring tolerance of my years of visiting the establishments of which I write (in the name of research!) gave me the encouragement I needed. I therefore dedicate this book to Ann-Marie.*

# Introduction

In Baines' County Directory of 1825 the following Whitefield inns and licensees are listed. **Besses o'th' Barn Tavern**, John Tanner; **Bull's Head,** Daniel Charlton; **Eagle and Child**, Higher Lane, Charles Holt; **Masons Arms**, Four Lane Ends, John Dawson; **Wheatsheaf**, Edward Partington.

## The 1830 Beerhouse Act

This Act was introduced in an attempt to curtail the consumption of gin and other spirits. This enabled any householder who was on the Rate Register to sell 'beer only' simply by paying two Guineas to the Excise Office. Permitted opening times were from 4am to 10pm (except during Divine Service on Sunday, Christmas Day and Boxing Day).

By 1838 there were nine public houses in Whitefield, the new ones being **The Derby Arms**, **Church Inn**, **William IV** and the **Brown Mare** on Higher Lane. There were also nineteen beerhouses.

Besides these licensed premises there were also dozens of illegal Houses known as 'hush shops'. Hole Bottom Farm (now part of Whitefield golf course) was said to have been a hush shop where the local weavers of the Park Lane area would go for a drink on the quiet.

In 1852 the population of Whitefield was 12,861 and there were now nineteen public houses and twenty four beerhouses. By 1899, however, Whitefield was down to only fifteen public houses and half a dozen beerhouses. It is almost certain that this massive reduction was a result of the **Wine and beerhouse Act of 1869** which required a Justice's certificate to obtain an Excise Licence for beerhouses and wine shops as well as for public houses. This tighter control of licences, coupled with the later Act of 1872 which introduced stricter restrictions on opening times for public houses and beerhouses brought about the demise of many of them.

## 1904 Compensation Act

The next legislation that affected pubs and beerhouses dramatically was the 1904 Compensation Act. This allowed Licensing Magistrates to refer for compensation and effectively close any premises whose licence they considered unsuitable or unnecessary and many establishments were closed down simply because it was considered there were too many in proximity to each other. This was certainly the case with several Whitefield pubs.

In the seventy years between the 1880s and 1950s Whitefield lost at least fourteen of its public houses and beerhouses, some to slum clearance and some to road making schemes. Others were lost due to decline in business through difficult times and some as a direct result of the 1904 Compensation Act.

It is my desire to attempt to bring these lost pubs back, albeit only in these pages. Most of them have long been forgotten yet they all played their part in the Whitefield of bygone days and if for that one reason alone it is proper that they are remembered. The Black Horse Inn and the Victoria Inn, for example, may both be long gone (see pages 16/17), but surely they will both be long remembered, along with Whitefield's other lost pubs.

It was my original intention to call this book the 'History of Pilkington Pubs' but Pilkington was a very vast area and it would have taken several volumes to document even the briefest histories of every beerhouse and public house spread over such a large area.

I have therefore reached a compromise by keeping to the Whitefield area as we know it today, but including three Unsworth pubs and two which sit on the Whitefield urban district boundary with Prestwich.

Twenty-two present day public houses are therefore covered alongside twelve of the the lost pubs, making a total of thirty-four. Most of them are very old with rich and fascinating histories; a few are young but have great historical connections. The district also had two breweries and an account of them is also given.

Where it has been possible to obtain photographs of distant past and relatively recent landlords and landladies and some of their customers, they have been included. I would have liked to have included more but had I gone on searching indefinitely for such material this work would never have come to fruition.

Of the twenty-two present day pubs listed I have been frequenting most of them at various times for almost thirty years. Throughout those years I have not only enjoyed the ale and hospitality, but have also enjoyed enormously the pubs themselves. I hope you enjoy reading about them.

Glenn Worth, Whitefield, 1993.

**Glenn Worth, during research for this book**

*A History of Whitefield Pubs*

# The Earliest Surviving Alehouse Recognizance for Pilkington

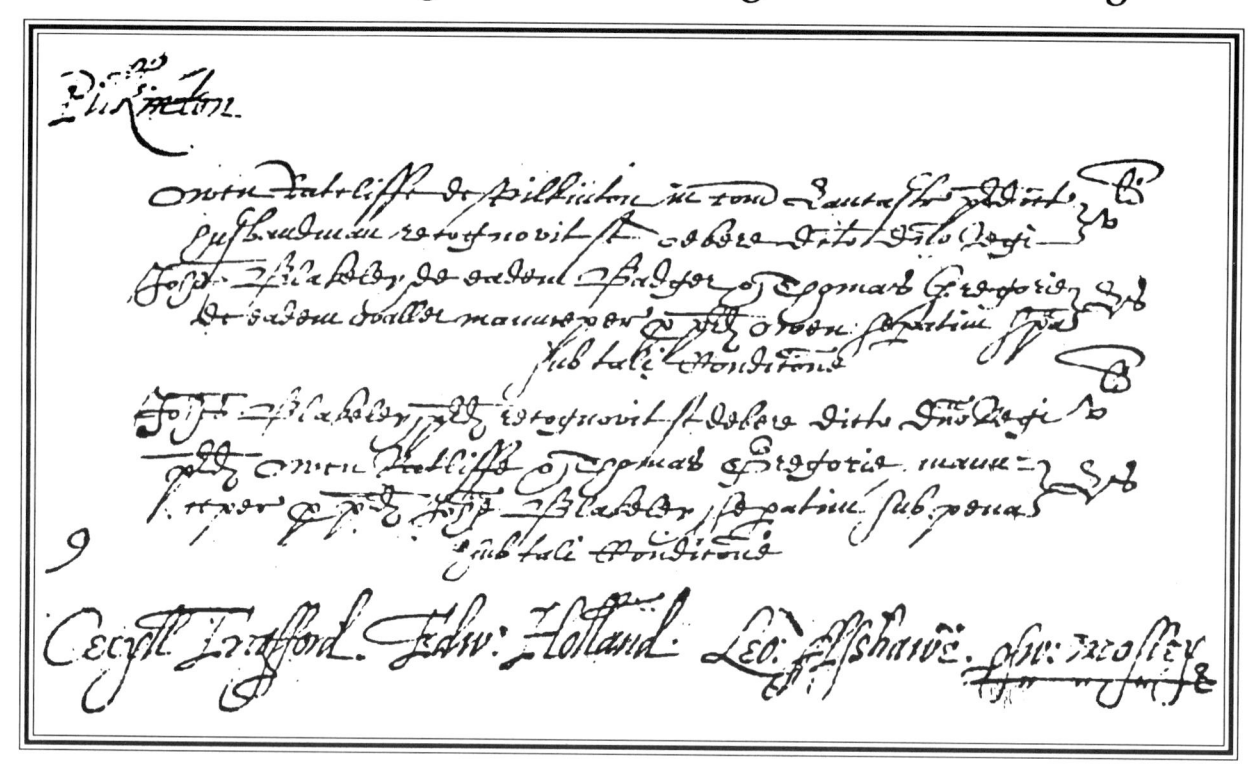

The first two known beer sellers in Pilkington were **Owen Ratcliffe** and **John Blakeley**. Their names are found in the earliest surviving recognizance for Pilkington dated 1629 (shown above). This was an early Licensing Register. A word for word translation follows.

*Owen Ratcliffe of Pilkington in the county of Lancaster aforesaid, husbandman, acknowledges himself to owe our aforesaid Lord the King - £5.*

*John Blakeley of the same, Badger and Thomas Gregorie of the same, Waller, sureties for the aforesaid separately under the pain of 50 shillings. Upon the same condition.*

*John Blakeley aforesaid acknowledges himself to owe our aforesaid Lord the King - £5.*

*The aforesaid Owen Ratcliffe and Thomas Gregorie, sureties for the aforesaid John Blakeley. Separately, under pain of 50 shillings. Upon the same condition.*

This simply means that Owen Ratcliffe was a farmer who pledged £5 to the King for his licence to sell ale. (Only to be paid if the licence is forfeited). John Blakely and Thomas Gregorie stand as surety against Owen's licence by pledging their 50 shillings each to the King. John Blakeley also wanted a licence and he pledged £5 to the King. Owen Ratcliffe (returning the favour) along with Thomas Gregorie now stand as surety against John's licence.

John Blakeley is described as a 'Badger'; this was the word used for dealers in corn. Thomas Gregorie is referred to as a 'Waller' who was a builder of walls. Each pledged 50 shillings to stand as sureties against Owen Ratcliffe's licence. The officials' names at the bottom are Cecyll Trafford, EDW Holland, Leo F Shaw, Tho. Mosley.

The recognizance makes no mention of where they lived (other than Pilkington) and at the time of writing it is not known from where they sold their beer.

*Stage coach days, Besses toll house*

Page 6

A History of Whitefield Pubs

A section of William Yates map of Lancashire 1786 showing the constituent districts of Pilkington which were Whitefield, Outwood, Stand, Ringley, Unsworth, Hollins and Besses o'th' Barn

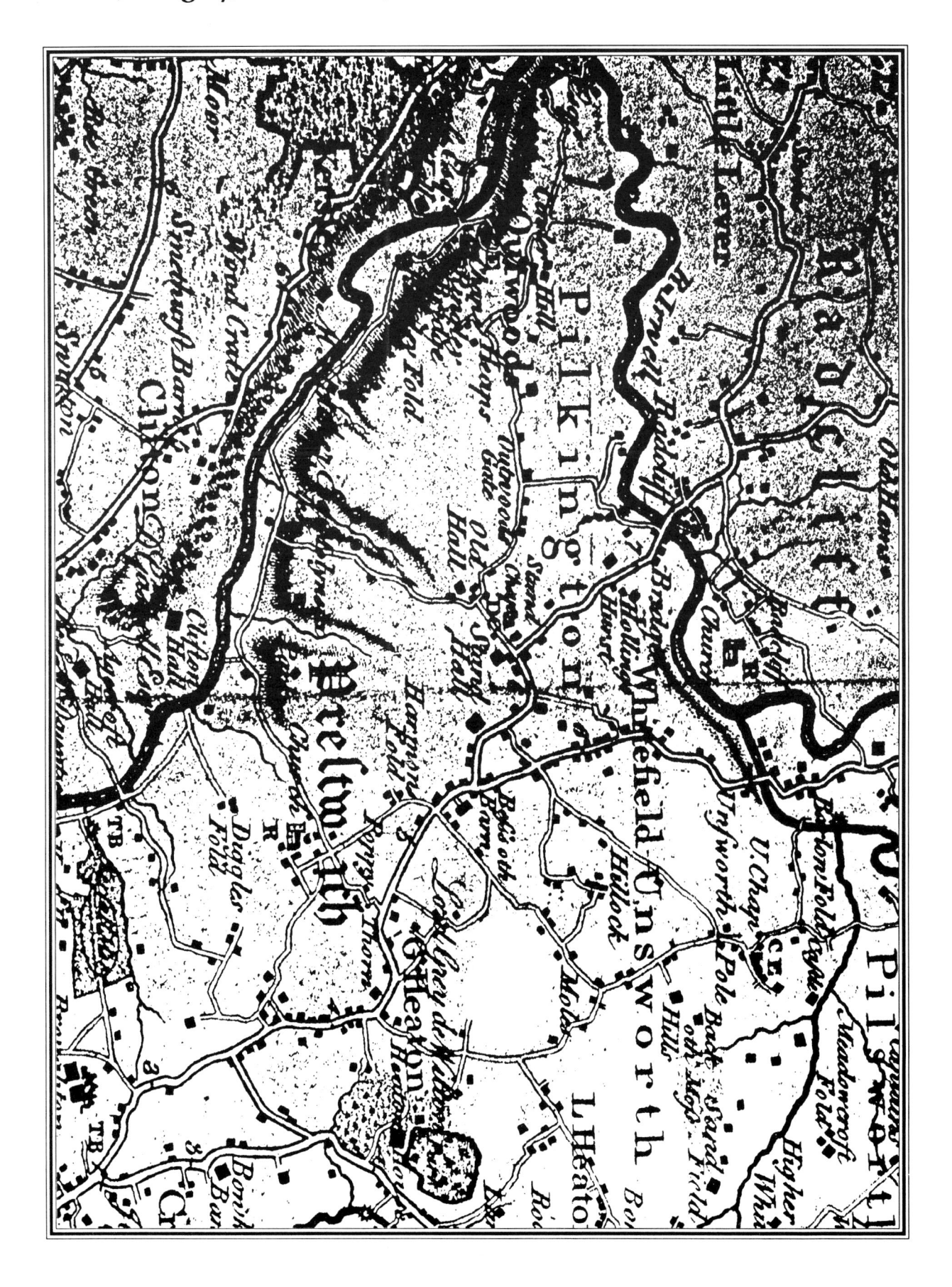

*A History of Whitefield Pubs*

# Albert Inn

## Ribble Drive/Oak Lane

Built in 1817 and once a secluded Tudor-style country pub, the Albert Inn became the 'local' for many residents who were housed on the new Hillock Estate in the early 1960s.

At that time the Albert was the only pub in the centre of the estate. The last licensee at the old inn was Robert Warrington and his wife who had been customers for fifteen years before they took over in 1966.

Right from the early days there appears to have been a quick succession of Tenants with a current total to date of 48; of these only five have held the licence for five years or more and they were Mary Jackson, Fred Farrer, Frank March, Samuel Kendal and the longest serving so far, Edward Pool (1940 to 1956).

In 1849 the property sited on the land was referred to as a dwelling house and a Mr George Fletcher with another sold it to Mr Thomas Wroe. The conveyance for the sale is the earliest document on file.

In 1872 the property was still a private dwelling house but shortly afterwards it became a beerhouse. James Barlow is listed as the licensee in the early 1870s. Its first 'official' mention appears in 1883 where an entry in the deeds describes it as a beerhouse known by the name of 'General Jackson', the owner at the time being a Mr James Green.

In 1892 the premises were leased to Boddington's Brewery and still known as 'General Jackson'; by 1901, however, the name had changed to the 'Albert Inn' under the new ownership of Martha Hill. Martha sold it to Richard Seed and Company of Spring Lane Brewery Radcliffe in 1904. It is interesting to note that Martha was licensee of the Robin Hood on Higher Lane for twenty-one years (1883 to 1904) and must have acquired ownership of the Albert Inn some time between 1892 and 1901.

*The 'Original' Albert Inn. First known as The General Jackson*

Dutton's Blackburn Brewery Ltd bought the Albert from Richard Seed and Co on the 5th of December 1938. At that time the inn was described as 'beer on only'. According to the deeds the area of land and upon which the inn was sited was 622 square yards. In 1964 the Albert changed ownership again when Dutton's were taken over by Whitbread and Co along with 784 other licensed houses and the Albert became part of the Whitbread West Pennine Property Estate, a title which ceased in 1978.

*A closer look at the gable end showing the Dutton's sign*

In 1967 the old inn was demolished and a new licensed 'Albert Hotel' was built at the side of it; the extract from the architect's plans opposite clearly shows this change of site. Since the new Albert was built two applications for structural alterations have been made and granted, the first on the 26th July 1972 and the second on the 3rd of September 1980.

Nowadays the site is part leasehold and part freehold, the lease being for 99 years from 1st March 1963 and comprising approximately 3,025 square yards. The freehold is held under the terms of the conveyance (mentioned earlier) dated 5th December 1938 from Richard Seed & Co Limited to Dutton's Lancashire and Yorkshire Brewery Corporation Ltd. This freehold portion is the site of the original Albert Inn and now forms part of the car park.

> *How the name 'General Jackson' came about is a matter of conjecture. There was a General who served in the British army as a surgeon during the Crimean War. Another General Jackson was the American Confederate known as 'Stonewall'. Whether there was a local connection between either of these Generals is not yet known. Research continues on this matter.*

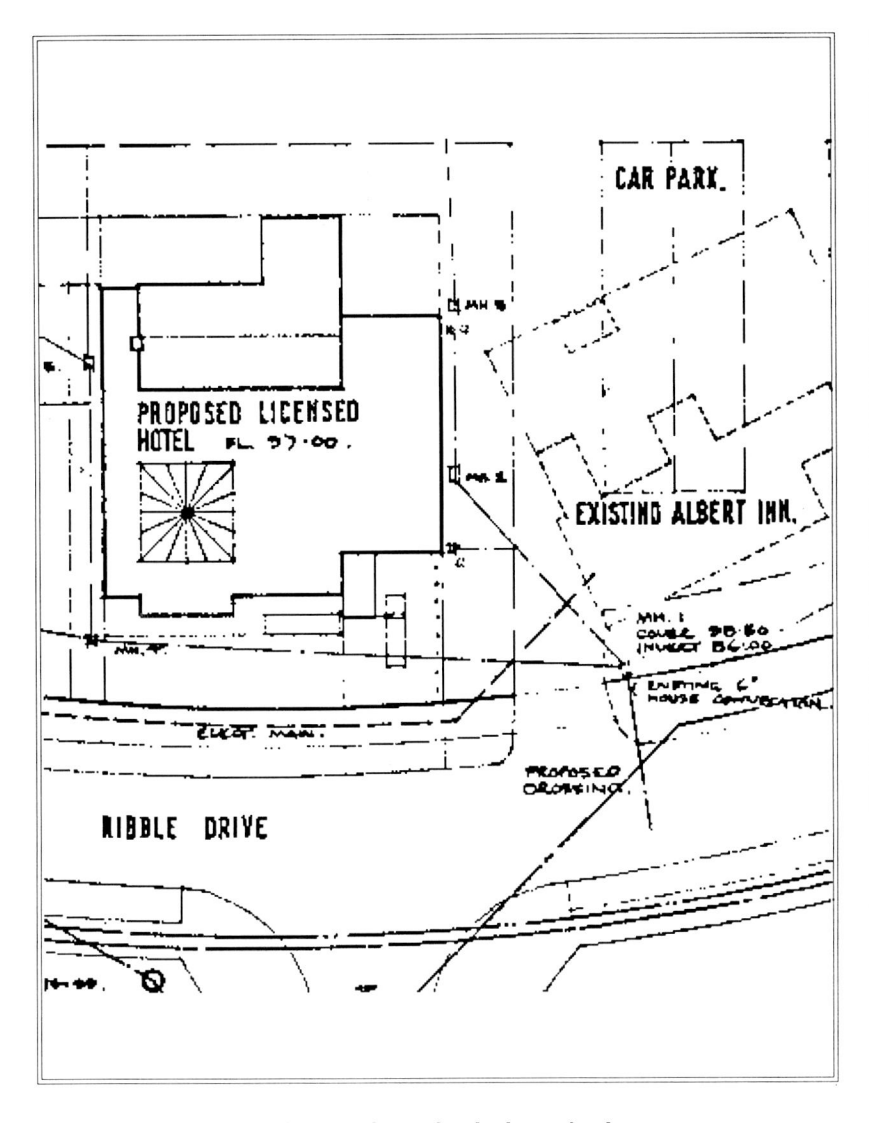

*Extract from the Architect's plan*

## Known Licensees

| | |
|---|---|
| James Barlow | 1870s |
| Robert Haslam | 31 8 1877 |
| William Haslam | 10 1 1878 |
| William Stott | 29 5 1879 |
| James Greaves | 29 9 1881 |
| Mary Greaves | 28 5 1885 |
| Mary Jackson | 8 7 1886 |
| John Bell | 3 11 1892 |
| William Ainsworth | 7 11 1901 |
| John Ellis Greaves | 18 1 1904 |
| Henry Hall | 14 9 1908 |
| Frank March | 2 5 1912 |
| Fred Farrar | 3 10 1918 |
| John Kershaw | 8 2 1923 |
| Mary Kershaw | 12 2 1925 |
| Samuel Kendal | 21 10 1929 |
| Ellen Kendall | 7 2 1935 |
| Henry Petty | 28 5 1936 |
| William Henry Wood | 25 4 1938 |
| Edward Pool | 30 12 1940 |
| Harold Asher | 22 10 1956 |
| Eric G Fry | 27 10 1958 |
| Patrick Connally | 8 12 1960 |
| Joseph W Walker | 1 6 1961 |
| William Holland | 23 7 1940 |
| William Hatch | 21 7 1965 |
| Robert Warrington | 4 4 1966 |
| Colin Leigh | 5 2 1968 |
| Robert Warrington | 10 11 1969 |
| Christopher Jones | 20 7 1970 |
| Charles Lucas | 6 12 1971 |
| Christopher Dalby | 15 3 1976 |
| James B Green | 20 7 1977 |
| Paul Robinson | 7 12 1977 |
| Leonard Bamber | 30 4 1980 |
| Barry Brook | 15 10 1980 |
| Frank Jackson | 4 9 1940 |
| Robert Bingham | 23 2 1982 |
| Robert Halewood | 29 10 1982 |
| Stephen Butler | 19 10 1983 |
| John Barton | 29 10 1985 |
| Alan Davies | 9 12 1986 |
| Harry Pace | 7 12 1988 |
| Dorothy Bland | 25 8 1990 |
| John Grieveson | 24 10 1990 |
| David Busnell | 24 7 1991 |
| Alan Davies | 29 4 1992 |
| Carl Vincent Healey | 10 3 1993 |

It is now 176 years since the predecessor to the 'Albert' (Albert, Prince consort to Queen Victoria) appeared on Oak Lane and many changes have taken place, one of which in more recent years is again the name of the place. On the 9th December 1986 the pub was officially renamed the 'Prince Albert'.

At the time of writing the Prince Albert is leased by Whitbread to Wolverhampton & Dudley Breweries, the largest surviving independent brewer in the country and is selling Banks's beers.

## Interesting facts

*On the 18th June 1871 James Barlow, the landlord was found to be serving ale at 7.25am on Sunday morning. On the 27th June he appeared at Bury before Captain K Mellor the Magistrate and was fined £5 plus costs.*

*Henry Petty who was Landlord (1936-1938) liked women so much that he married two of them and was charged with bigamy.*

**The Prince Albert with Banks's Livery (Photo 1991)**

*A History of Whitefield Pubs*

# Besses o'th' Barn Inn  Bury Old Road

*Photograph A: The original old inn and bowling green circa 1882*

The Besses o'th' Barn Inn was a classic example of a public house which served the local community, as well as providing rest and refreshment for weary travellers. It was the meeting place for several societies and a variety of sporting events were held there. Its rooms were used for auctions and other public meetings and before Whitefield had its own Post Office the inn was a collection and delivery point for mail. In the depression years of the 1930s and not long before it closed, the inn served as a different kind of collection point, for cast off clothing donated for poor children of the district.

The earliest landlord who can be traced to the Besses o'th' Barn Inn was John Fallows. He took the licence in 1715, when he was thirty years old and stayed for some forty-two years. During his time there the inn was occasionally mentioned in newspaper advertisements. On the 19th January 1748, for instance, the Manchester Magazine contained a notice inviting the creditors of Charles Ashworth, a linen weaver of Stand, to meet Mr Ashworth's assignees at the inn in order to collect their share of his effects.

In the same newspaper on the 6th March 1749, an auction was advertised '*At the house of John Fallows, known by the name of Besses o'th' Barn, in Pilkington*'. The property for sale was Smedley Mills '*consisting of housing, out-housing, twelve acres of land. A water corn mill and kiln and a paper mill*' (The Manchester Magazine was a weekly newspaper and as the forerunner to the Manchester Mercury, another weekly that started publication in March 1752 up until 1830).

John Fallows was succeeded by Alice Fallows (his widow?) in 1758. Then another John Fallows (their son?) kept the inn for one year in 1764.

*Photograph B: The inn circa 1888 after extensive alterations*

Over the years there has been much speculation as to the origin of the name of this famous inn, which in the course of time became the name of the district. The most fanciful that has been bandied about for many years is that highwayman Dick Turpin once stabled his horse, Black Bess, there. Apart from the fact that Mr Turpin conducted his business nowhere near Whitefield, the name Besses o'th' Barn was already established when Black Bess was learning to walk! The most plausible explanation is that a lady called Bess kept the inn, there was a barn nearby and both became well known local landmarks. Seventeenth century Licensing records are incomplete, but they show that for most of that period there were between two and six ale house keepers in the Pilkington area. Only two of all those listed were named Elizabeth and the likely candidate for Bess is Elizabeth Bamford, who kept an inn or ale house between the years 1674 and 1699.

Ale house names and addresses are not listed in these early records, but in view of later evidence it is possible that Bess's inn had the sign of the dog. In 1765 George Horrocks took over the inn after the Fallows family left and during his time there registered the name 'Dog Inn' at the annual Licensing meetings. It would have been Besses o'th' Barn to local people and travellers alike, so maybe George was using a formal name established over a century before. He ran the inn until 1818 and in doing so established himself as the longest serving landlord that Whitefield has ever had, with fifty-three years continuous service. **He created a record unequalled to this day.**

*Extract from the Manchester Magazine 19th January 1748*

*Extract from the Manchester Magazine 6th March 1749*

**OCTOBER 28th, 1932**
WHITEFIELD Footwear Fund made an appeal for cast-off children's clothing. The announcement said: As a large number of children in the district are at present insufficiently clothed owing to the trade depression, clothes could be sent to the Besses o' th' Barn Hotel, and other addresses.

☆

*From a local newspaper*

John Tanner was the next known landlord who also owned the property. A directory published in 1818 lists the inn as the 'Bowling Green', which suggests that the green had been laid out about then. By 1821 the pub is listed as the Besses o'th' Barn Tavern, a name which it kept with some minor variations for well over a century.

A room in the old barn next to the inn, known as the 'mangle room' (usually where washing was done) was the original practice place for the world famous Besses o'th' Barn Band between 1818, and 1827 when the old barn was demolished and replaced with stables.

There followed a succession of licensees between the 1830s and 1870s about whom little is known. We do find from records, however, that during Samuel Johnson's tenancy (circa 1864-1877), the owner of the inn was listed as Edward J Hampson, 90 King Street, Manchester.

*An unusual feature of the inn was the 'Monkey room' where some stuffed monkeys were displayed in a glass showcase. The inn was also a meeting place for the local soap sellers who would gather there before going on their door-to-door rounds.*

*A History of Whitefield Pubs*

**Photograph C: The Besses o'th' Barn Band and the Newcastle Steel Works Band from Australia outside the Besses o'th Barn Hotel in 1924**

Richard Morris became the licensee in September 1878 and he can be seen in the 1882 photograph (A), standing in the doorway in his white coat. This photograph shows the inn a few years before extensive alterations were made. They consisted of the gable (facing front and pinned) being removed, sagging roof timbers replaced, the roof reslated and the whole frontage changed. By comparing photographs A and B, it can be seen that the original doorway became a window, the window to the right of the door was turned into a doorway and an additional window was made on the right. To complete the transformation, roof sign boards (or skyboards) were put up.

During the late 19th century, Whitefield Wakes, a very popular local event, used to take place on a field at the side of the inn. It was said that once the 'Wakes Men' had set up their stalls they would empty their water barrel, take it across to the inn and have it filled up with ale.

Around the same time, rugby was very popular in the Whitefield area. Two teams, the Whitefield Rangers and Whitefield Albion used a room at the inn for changing when they played on the pitch on Thatch Leach Lane (nowadays covered by houses). No doubt many a pint of ale was downed in the inn afterwards!

The Besses o'th' Barn Inn gained another sporting connection when John Harrison became landlord in July 1886. John and his son James were members of the Salford Harriers and for some years the club occasionally made the inn the starting point for a run. Unfortunately, John Harrison was charged with permitting drunkenness and appeared before the Magistrates Colonel Mellor, J Whittaker, H Openshaw and J Aitken at Bury Courthouse on 26th March 1888 and was fined 20 shillings plus costs. He was back in court on the 14th July 1890 for the same offence, this time appearing before Magistrates Wrigley, Aitken, Young and Hazel. This time they doubled the fine to 40 shillings plus costs.

It is quite possible that John Harrison was sacked because of this last conviction as he was replaced by Henry Greenhalgh shortly afterwards (the inn at the time was still owned by Edward Hampson of King St Manchester).

In November 1889 a report was prepared by the Chief Constable to ascertain the number of public houses in each Licensing division. The general condition and accommodation facilities of each fully licensed house, the ability to cater for travellers requiring accommodation and refreshment other than drink, stabling provisions and the distance from the two nearest fully licensed public houses.

Besses o'th' Barn Inn was registered as having two spare beds, facilities to feed up to 100 persons and stabling for eight horses and was 210 yards (Beehive) and 450 yards (Coach and Horses) from the next two fully licensed houses.

In 1908 Edward Holt acquired the property for Joseph Holt's Brewery, the first Holt's tenant being James Hutton. A section of the proposed contract to purchase reads *'Land on the north easterly side of Bury Old Road, Besses o'th' Barn, Whitefield, containing 4,600 superficial square yards or thereabouts with a frontage of 66 yards 2 inches, together*

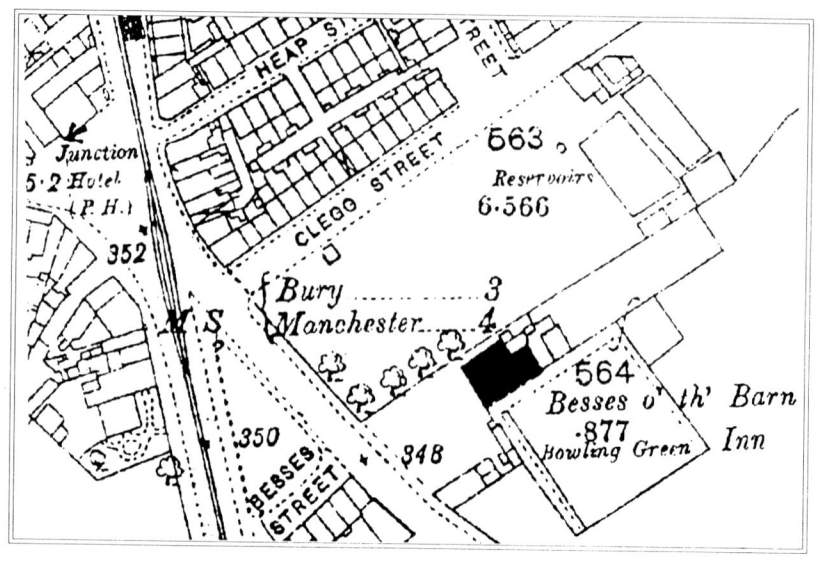

**An extract from the 1883 Ordnance Survey map of Besses Junction showing the inn and bowling green**

Page 12

*with the public house known as Besses o'th' Barn Inn and other buildings erected thereon'.*

The Hutton family were to run the inn for the next sixteen years ending with Johnny Hutton, whose name can be seen over the door on the photograph with the bands outside which was taken in 1924, the year he left.

Around 1924 the word 'Inn' on the skyboards was changed to 'Hotel', although this was to be short lived as the building only lasted another 15 years.

*Salford Harriers' fixture list for 1896. They met at the inn 15th February*

### Known Licensees

| | |
|---|---|
| John Tanner | 1715 |
| Alice Fallows | 1758 |
| John Fallows | 1764 |
| George Horrocks | 1765 |
| John Tanner | 1818 |
| Anne Edge | 1830s - 40s |
| Robert Tanner | 1850s |
| George Wood | (approx) 1858 |
| Samuel Johnson | (approx) 1864 |
| Eliza Johnson | 3 9 1877 |
| Richard Morris | 30 9 1878 |
| Robert Gordon | 29 3 1883 |
| Jessie Gordon | 10 1 1884 |
| Thomas Dauneas | 26 5 1885 |
| John Harrison | 8 7 1886 |
| Henry Greenhalgh | 11 12 1890 |
| John Beswick | 5 11 1891 |
| Enos Gladstone | 26 3 1894 |
| Benjamin Mawdsley | 7 1 1899 |
| James R Fowler | 29 3 1899 |
| James H Hutton | 27 7 1908 |
| Ellen Hutton | 4 9 1913 |
| Johnny Hutton | 4 12 1916 |
| Charles Sandiford | 20 10 1924 |
| Jesse Dodd | 3 1 1926 |
| Cicely Dodd | 18 10 1926 |
| Albert E O'Shea | 25 7 1927 |
| Ernest H Newly | 6 5 1929 |
| Lapse of Licence | 5 1 1935 |

The pub's last ever licensee was Ernest Newly, whose tenancy ran from 6th May 1929 until 5th January 1935, when the licence lapsed under the 1904 Compensation Act. Newly replaced Albert O'Shea who was, in all probability, sacked by Holts as he was convicted on 22nd April 1929 at Radcliffe, on seven counts of allowing the sale of liquor outside the permitted licensing hours. It is highly unlikely to be pure coincidence that Newly's tenancy commenced just a fortnight after the hearing. A letter sent to Holts dated the 24th April from the Magistrates confirms O'Shea's conviction.

*Photograph D: Just before demolition started in 1939*

*Photograph E: Whitefield Ambulance Station taken in 1992*

Photograph D shows the hotel just before it was demolished in 1939. The old stables (right of picture) had become a garage and workshop owned by a Mr Barnicle who lived in Blackley. At the time this photograph was taken he sold petrol at 1s. 11d. per gallon (9p). Whitefield Ambulance Station (shown in photograph E) now stands on what was the bowling green of the old inn and coincidentally faces the same way is the inn itself once did.

*A History of Whitefield Pubs*

# The Bull's Head

## Bury New Road

The Bull's Head has been improved from time to time over the years but looks little different from 100 years ago.

From old directories we learn that in 1818 Thomas Roe was listed as a victualler at the Bull's Head (which means it is likely he was brewing on the premises). Daniel Charlton in 1825, William Smith in 1843, Joseph Place in 1850, followed by Thomas Entwistle 1858-1861.

As local licensing magistrates' records only date back to 1869, the further back we go the more difficult it becomes to trace landlords and owners. A search of the old census returns and Rate registers is also hampered by the fact that the inn signs are rarely mentioned in these old records. It is also difficult to determine exactly how long known licensees were at any one place as many directories no longer exist. So, for example, a licensee may only be identified by a single directory entry and it is almost impossible to give precise dates of tenancy as a result.

*Photograph A: Bulls Head in the early 1960s. Note the Dutton's signs*

However, despite difficulties tracing records, the next known licensee after Thomas Entwistle to take charge was quite easy to identify. He was Thomas Wardle and apart from holding the licence at the Bull's Head, he also owned a tailor's shop at number one, Higher Lane. He appears on a photograph taken outside the Travellers Inn (included in this publication, page 92/3).

The earliest reference in the deeds is the year 1887 when the land and property is shown as being in the possession of the Earl of Derby. The land and property was conveyed to the Crown Brewing Co on the 8th November 1921. It remained in their ownership until they sold '*740 square yards of land with the Bull's Head on site*' to Dutton's Brewery Ltd of Blackburn on the 22nd of March 1960.

Shown on the left is a photocopy of the plan annexed to the conveyance dated 8th November 1921, the Earl of Derby KG to the Crown Brewery Co Ltd. The 'intended' street on the plan is now Devon Street.

The Chief Constable's Report of 1889 (described fully in Besses o'th' Barn text) describes the Bull's Head as having no spare beds; could feed 30 persons; stabling facilities for 30 horses(!) and 90 yards and 60 yards from the two nearest public houses.

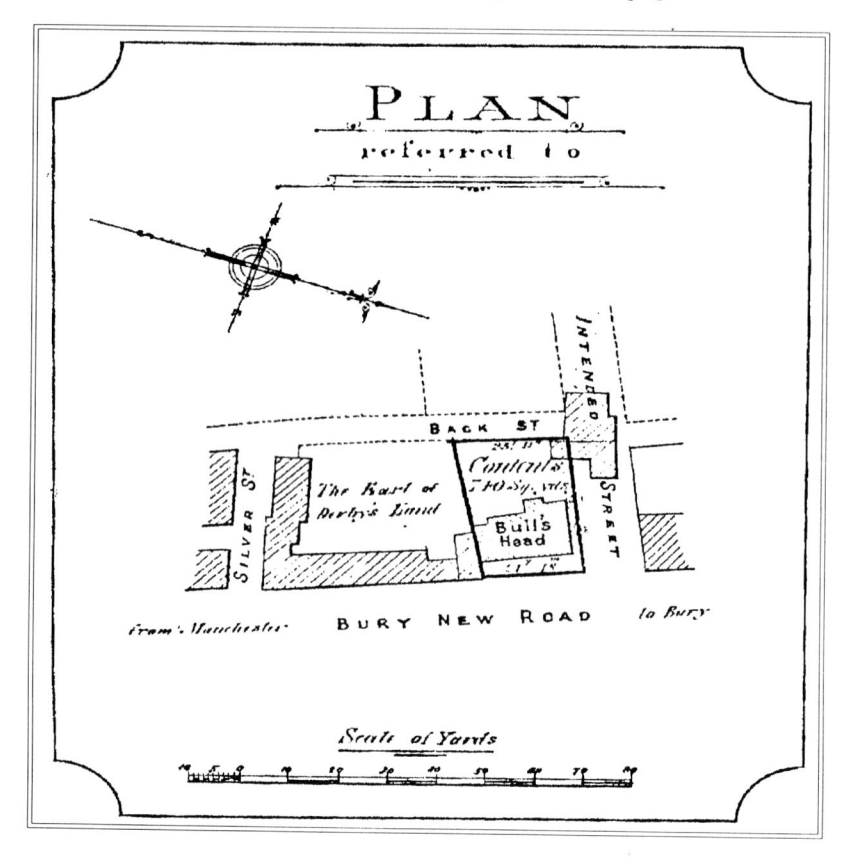

Events in 1819 which later became known as the 'Peterloo Massacre' are recalled here, having a bearing on the history of the Bull's Head. Among the 61,000 reformers led to St. Peter's fields (now St Peter's Square) by Samuel Bamford, the Middleton weaver, was a contingent from Park Lane and another from Lily Hill. When the reformers set off from Whitefield, the landlord of the Bull's Head supporting the reformers, brought out a barrel of ale for them, but the landlord of the Wheatsheaf on the side of Church and King, put up his shutters and barricaded his doors. Despite the threats of the reformers and pleading of his neighbours, he would not allow any ale to leave his cellar.

The photograph of the Bull's Head on the right is taken from the site of the old Victoria Inn. The building to the left of the picture was once the Black Horse Inn (currently occupied by a firm of solicitors and a firm of surveyors). Green Lane ran between the two pubs. The fourth concrete stump from the left is approximately where the front door to the Victoria Inn would have been. The rear of this site now houses the 'Fisherman's Wharf' restaurant and the Elms Square shopping centre.

*Photograph B: The Bull's Head July 1991 (Compare photos A & B)*

### Known Licensees

| | |
|---|---|
| Thomas Roe | 1818 |
| Daniel Charlton | 1825 |
| William Smith | 1843 |
| Joseph Place | 1850 |
| Thomas Entwisle | 1858 |
| Thomas Wardle | 1883 |
| Edwin Holt | 2 9 1895 |
| William Houghton | 14 1 1897 |
| Thomas Woodburn | 12 2 1900 |
| John Robinson | 18 3 1901 |
| William Lightbown | 3 11 1902 |
| Sara Ann Lightbown | 25 10 1906 |
| John Lightbown | 7 2 1907 |
| Ellen Lightbown | 8 3 1928 |
| John Bently | 3 12 1931 |
| Joseph Bartle | 5 3 1936 |
| Smith Kershaw | 10 10 1938 |
| William Oddie | 26 5 1949 |
| Stuart Malpas | 7 2 1952 |
| Leslie Swift | 5 6 1958 |
| Llewellyn Jones | 14 4 1975 |
| S Murray | 10 7 1984 |
| Peter Kelly | 4 6 1985 |
| David Camilleri | 10 10 1985 |
| James McCalse | 27 10 1987 |

*The name 'Bull's Head' originates from the fact that during the Reformation Inn Keepers whose sign was the Pope's Head, which was quite a popular name in those days, quickly changed it. The favourite new sign was 'The King's Head', usually depicting Henry VIII. Some landlords who were loyal to Rome subtly hid their love of the old faith in their new signs. The 'Bull's Head' is an example of such hidden devotion to Rome.*

*A 'bull' is an edict or rescript of the Pope, published or transmitted to the Churches over which he is head, therefore any innkeeper showing the sign of the Bull's Head would no doubt be true to Rome.*

*Photograph C: A Crown Brewery House until 1960, the Bull's Head is now owned by Whitbread*

*Two Ken Greenhalgh paintings from the Bull, 'Fives and Three's' and 'Lonely Lady'*

*A History of Whitefield Pubs*

# Black Horse Inn incorporating the Victoria Inn

*Photograph A: The building still stands but has been altered beyond all recognition as an inn*

The popular inn sign, the Black Horse dates from the fourteenth century. Its use appears to be a reflection of its convenience as a visual symbol. By the 17th century the phrase had become the nickname of the 7th Dragoon Guards who had black collars and cuffs on their tunics and rode mainly black horses.

Whitefield's Black Horse Inn was owned by Joseph and Ann Bentley who also owned the Coach & Horses and the Cross Keys. The beer was supplied by the Bentley Brewery at Kirkhams. The inn appears to have come into existence around the mid 1860s as a beerhouse and was never fully licensed.

Along with the Coach & Horses and the Cross Keys, Ann Bentley (by now a widow) sold the Black Horse to Gustavus F Carrington in 1879 who at that time was expanding his business out of the Hulme district. In 1897 the Carrington family decided to sell up and all their licensed premises came up for sale at a public auction held at the 'Thatched House Hotel' in Manchester on the 27th July 1897. Most were acquired by the Manchester Brewery Company of Britannia Brewery, Brodie Street, Manchester (See also Coach & Horses text pp 39-42). They became part of Walker and Homfray, brewers of Salford in 1912, who in turn merged with Wilsons, Newton Heath brewery in 1949.

The photograph above shows the Black Horse (right of picture) circa 1910 with a young boy and a dog in the doorway. Bury New Road can be seen curling round to the right, Lily Hill Street is dead ahead and the Cross Keys can just be seen in the distance on the right hand side. Radcliffe New Road slips off to the left of the picture, past the old Telephone Exchange. The shop slightly left of the Black Horse, on the opposite corner of Green Lane was once the Victoria Inn. Unfortunately, very little is known about it. Despite extensive research, few facts have come to light. What is known is that it was referred for compensation under the 1904 Act circa 1905/6 when it closed as a beerhouse and shortly afterwards became Braddock's Grocers and later a greengrocer's.

*Photograph B: This was once the Victoria Inn, a beerhouse*

Page 16

The Black Horse Inn building, though now totally unrecognisable as an inn, still stands and is currently occupied by a firm of solicitors and a firm of surveyors. New windows and a doorway have been recently installed into the gable end onto what was once the section of Green Lane that used to open out into Bury New Road.

These premises along with the other dwellings on that curved section of Bury New Road were only demolished in the 1960s when Elms Square shopping centre and the Bell Waldron (now Fisherman's Wharf) restaurant were built.

Photograph C taken in 1991 from a similar position as D shows little change has taken place in 86 years. Regional Homes, the then occupiers of the building, can be seen next to the concrete stumps (site of the old Victoria Inn). The Wheatsheaf swinging sign can be seen in the distance

*Photograph C: Regional Homes, the then occupiers of the building which was once the Black Horse (taken in 1991)*

*Photograph D: Whit Friday 1907. New Jerusalem Church, Besses (Looking from Lily Hill Street)*

*Photograph E: Whit Friday 1906. The Black Horse Inn is left of the banner*

Photograph D shows the New Jerusalem Church procession, passing the Black Horse on Whit Friday 1907. Braddock's grocers, formerly the Victoria Inn, is just out of sight behind the banner. Observe the skyboards bearing the legend 'Manchester Brewery Co Ltd' down the gable apex on the Black Horse. The Derby Hotel can be seen in the right hand corner of the picture. Notice the two large gas lamps.

Photograph E shows the Stand Church procession passing the entrance to Radcliffe New Road. On this picture the Black Horse and Braddock's are both clearly visible.

The inn was referred for compensation in 1911 and the licence expired in December 1912 when the doors closed as a local hostelry for the very last time.

### Known Licensees

| | |
|---|---|
| John Entwistle | 1860s |
| Elisha Hampson | 3 6 1881 |
| Marshall Hampson | 13 9 1888 |
| Sara Jane Hampson | 28 8 1900 |
| Francis Hill | 6 9 1900 |
| Thomas Hill | 2 2 1905 |
| Hannah Hill | 15 1 1906 |
| Joseph Hodkinson | 3 2 1910 |
| (Closed December 1912) | |

*A History of Whitefield Pubs*

# The Bay Horse — Higher Lane

The first Bay Horse was affectionately known as '**spoil the fight inn**' and was situated at number 37 Higher Lane, opposite Whitefield Brewery (see pp 55-58). It came into being around 1830 as a beerhouse (beer only sales) in what had originally been an old cottage which stood slightly further back than the later, larger and purpose-built public house (photograph A) which was fully licensed and built around 1870.

> Not a lot is known about the earlier tenants of the original Bay Horse, but we do know that Jacob Greaves ran the place from the mid 1850s until 1861 when it seems his wife Susannah took over. We may infer that Jacob had died by then. Jacob is also listed in an old directory of 1850 as being tenant at the 'Brown Mare' which was further up Higher Lane, approximately half way between the Bay Horse and Eagle & Child (see pages 53/4).

The first owner and licensee at the new Bay Horse was Robert (Bob) Merriet and the beer came from JH Twiggs, of Manor Brewery Salford who also owned the original inn for some time. How Bob Merriet came into ownership of the new pub is not known, although we do know that the Salford Brewery continued to supply the pub with beer until he sold out in 1882 when Richard Seed & Co of the Spring Lane Brewery, Radcliffe, bought the inn and supplied the beer.

**Photograph A: The Bay Horse. One of Whitefield's lost pubs**

The photograph above must have been taken after 1940 as Mrs Lily Marshall (daughter-in-law of the then licensee) who kindly loaned the picture confirms that the house on the right of the pub wasn't there when she visited in 1940.

The gable end skyboards both read 'Bay Horse' and could be seen from a great distance in both directions. Note the tap just above the air brick (left) and the faded word 'Horses' just above the tap (magnification may be required).

In 1905 JG Swales & Co Ltd, Naval Brewery Salford became the new owners of the Bay Horse and retained possession. 'Swales' Swill' as it was commonly referred to was a very popular 'pint' in those days despite the title bestowed upon it.

**Photograph B: The bar in 1952**

*Photograph C: Hilda's Tap Room leaving party*

At the rear of the Bay Horse was Pump Street and Briggs Square. A slum area where the inhabitants lived in deplorable conditions.

> Years ago the pub was the gathering place for the fighting men of Pump Street and its surrounds. Here it was considered the correct thing to get drunk on Saturday night and settle an argument with a good old stand up fight.
>
> Some nights there were as many as three or four sets of 'combatants' and they were not always just men! One man whose name has been lost in the passage of time was credited with 29 battles of which he had only won one, and drawn one.

Many amusing tales have survived about the locals of this notorious inn who lived in Pump Street. In the first house on the right hand side lived a man known as 'Yowler' who kept a truck cote, that is, he sold or exchanged pigeons.

'Yowler' had them so often that they used to return to him after every sale. One customer who was determined to stop this had pulled the flight feathers out of a pigeon he had bought so that it could not fly far, nevertheless it turned up back at Yowler's in a day or two with blisters on its feet, having walked all the way from Pendlebury; at least that was the tale!

A debt collector known as 'Old Stott' had many clients in this street. At one house he was paid a shilling a week which was placed on the table for him. His habit was to grab it quickly which did not please the woman who paid it.

One day she placed it on the fire shovel and got it hot over the fire. When she heard Stott's footsteps she slipped it on the table. Stott grabbed the shilling as usual but soon let go and heard the woman say that would teach him not to be so greedy.

In the early 1870s Jane Schofield held the licence and she was followed by Peter Warburton who took charge on 11th January 1875. With six pubs along this stretch of Higher Lane and a much smaller and less affluent population than nowadays, competition was fierce and landlords, rather than refuse business quite often took a chance. Peter Warburton did just that and was caught selling ale on Sunday. It seems it may not have been the first time as the licence was forfeited and the inn closed down.

Harry Kag took over shortly afterwards and the licence was renewed. By 1881 Nathan Crompton (previous owner of the Robin Hood) was the new licensee. A census return for that year declared Nathan Crompton, age 51, publican, place of birth, Yorkshire. His wife, Cecelia, aged 45, housekeeper, born Pilkington. His two daughters, Ada aged 10 and Annie aged 9 along with his son John aged 8, are all listed as scholars, Pilkington. It is interesting to note that in the Barret's Directory of 1883 Nathan is also listed as being a builder and contractor.

He was followed by Sarah Ann Clough, who also fell foul of the law and was charged with supplying drink to a constable while he was on duty and appeared at Bury

*Photograph D: Besses Junior AFC outside the Bay Horse 1931/2 season*

Courthouse before Magistrates Wrigley and Brierly esquires on 28th July 1887. The records say that she was ordered to pay costs, but the amount of any fine is not recorded. In any event, she was replaced almost two months later which leaves us to ponder whether she was ordered to forfeit her licence. The fact that her replacement, Mary Ward, was not there very long is perhaps an indication that a temporary stand-in was appointed until a more suitable tenant was found.

There followed a quite rapid succession of another 17 licensees before the Bay Horse was to find stability again. That came in the form of Joseph Hirst Marshall and his wife Rosette, who, with the help of their family, ran the place well from 1924 up until 1952. Photograph (B) shows Joseph and Rosette in the bar serving a pint (of what looks like mild) to Dan Howarth who was their son-in-law.

In September of 1952, their daughter Hilda Marshall took over the licence. It was to be a very short 'term of office' as landlady because soon afterwards the pub was referred for compensation upon payment of which the licence expired in 1953. Photograph C shows Hilda (standing and wearing glasses) at a leaving party she gave for her friends, in what is believed to be a presentation of a handbag by Peggy Leach and an umbrella from her mother, on behalf of all of them.

Besses Junior Amateur Football Club used to change in the Bay Horse and photograph D shows the team outside during the 1931-32 season. Joseph Marshall is stood on the pub steps at the back

> MR. and Mrs. JOSEPH H. MARSHALL, of the Bay Horse Hotel, Higher-lane, Whitefield, celebrated their diamond wedding yesterday. Four sons, four daughters, seven grandchildren and two great grandchildren attended the party.
> Mr. Marshall is 80, his wife 82, and they were married at Springside Methodist Chapel, Todmorden, on June 25, 1892. Mr. Marshall has kept the Bay Horse since 1924 and is considered to be the oldest licensee in the district. Forty years ago he took his family from Todmorden to Radcliffe where he got a job as a mill foreman.

**Extract from the Evening Chronicle, June 26th 1952**

**Photograph E: The dilapidated former Bay Horse just before demolition**

of the group. Some of their achievements were League Champions and Challenge Cup winners 1930-31 season, League Champions and Challenge Cup runners-up 1931-32 season. Their trophies were displayed in the bar.

After the pub had become delicensed in 1953, the building became the 'Sefton Social Club' and later a judo and weight lifting club. In 1963 the doors closed for the very last time and in 1965 the grand old building was demolished.

After leaving the pub, Hilda Marshall moved into a house nearby in Wilton Street and sadly she died in 1988. Hilda was also in her eighties.

### The Salford Brewery

*In 1895, the Salford Brewery merged with the Rochdale and Oldham Brewery Co to form the Rochdale and Manor Brewery Ltd. They were taken over by Samuel Smiths of Tadcaster in 1948.*

*The Salford Brewery had also supplied another pub in the area, the Commercial Inn at Heaton Park until 1894 when that pub was bought by the Worsley Brewery*

Pump Street had been changed to Fountain Street and when the area was demolished in 1937, residents were re-housed on the Victoria estate. Fountain Street has now long gone with the developments of the last thirty years but Fountain Place has sprung up near the old inn site (Manchester A to Z p29 - f2) and remains as part of the memories as do the stories of those hectic nights at the '**spoil the fight inn**'.

**Photograph F: The name lives on**

### Known Licensees

| | |
|---|---|
| Jacob Greaves | 1850s |
| Susannah Greaves | 1860s |
| Robert Merriet | early 1870s |
| Jane Schofield | 1872 |
| Peter Warburton | 11 1 1875 |
| Harry Kag | late 1870s |
| Nathan Crompton | 1880s |
| Sarah Ann Clough | 30 9 1886 |
| Mary Ward | 29 9 1887 |
| George H Clogg | 10 11 1887 |
| Henry Herbert Walsh | 17 1 1889 |
| Eliza Cessin | 4 11 1889 |
| Robert Eastwood | 27 3 1890 |
| Sarah Ann Smith | 3 11 1890 |
| Emma Smith | 22 5 1893 |
| Sarah Ann Thorpe | 2 7 1896 |
| Hannah Proctor | 4 12 1899 |
| George Alfred Roe | 16 7 1903 |
| James Carroll | 22 9 1904 |
| Joseph Howard Pollitt | 28 10 1909 |
| William John Lamb | 17 10 1910 |
| Joseph Samuel Evans | 4 5 1911 |
| Lucinda Bennett | 2 5 1912 |
| Fred Berry | 21 7 1913 |
| James Kinsey | 14 12 1918 |
| Annie Kinsey | 25 10 1920 |
| Joseph Hirst Marshall | 4 12 1924 |
| Hilda Marshall | 22 9 1952 |

**Photograph G: A view from the corner of Sefton Street nowadays (May 1992). The front door of the Bay Horse was where the pillar box is now.**

### Swales' Brewery

Swales' Brewery had its origins in a James Wheater who had a small brewery in Greenbank in Salford known as the Victoria Brewery.

For reasons best known to himself, Wheater tried to let the Brewery in 1851. His advertisement in the Manchester Guardian that year said '*To let, small brewery comprising steam engine, counting house, malt and hop rooms, cellars, yard and stabling for three horses. A good house is attached, well supplied with good springwater*'. The advert stated that the brewery output was 70 to 100 barrels per week.

There were, however, no takers and Wheater continued to run the brewery himself until 1857 when he took on a partner named James Clowes to form Wheater and Clowes, Victoria Brewery, Salford.

Around 1863 this partnership dissolved and Mr Clowes left the business. Shortly afterwards Mr Wheater found himself another partner in Mr Swales to form Wheater and Swales.

**Swales bottle label**

On the 6th August 1891, the firm became a Registered Company under the title of J G Swales and Co Ltd (see skyboards on photograph A) but remained a family business.

In 1899/1900 they moved to Hulme, taking over the old Cardwell and Co Naval Brewery. It was at the time that Mr Swales gained overall control of the business, which continued to prosper.

In 1950, one of the two Swales family members on the Board, Mr R Swales was listed as being Chairman, Managing director, Secretary and Head Brewer!

Boddington's bought out and closed Swales' Brewery in 1971, along with the 38 pubs and 6 off-licences the company owned.

We can reflect that had the Bay Horse and the Robin Hood survived, there would now be two Boddington's pubs on Higher Lane.

# Public House Terms

The following is a list of commonly used terms in the licensed trade, some of which are misused by the layperson.

## Barrel

A barrel is a cask of 36 gallons and this is also the unit in which beer outputs and sales are recorded.

Outside the trade, the word 'barrel' is often used to describe all sorts of containers for beers. This is understandable but not strictly correct and in the brewing and pub world the general reference would be 'casks' (or kegs in the case of pressurised beers). While a barrel is 36 gallons, other sizes of casks are

- Pin: 4½ gallons
- Firkin: 9 gallons
- Kilderkin: 18 gallons
- Hogshead: 54 gallons
- Puncheon: 72 gallons (not used any more)
- Butt: 108 gallons (not used any more)

These are English sizes; Scottish, Irish and American volumes are different for the same terms. Keg measures are commonly 11 gallons and 22 gallons; these are metric equivalents of 50 and 100 litres.

## Beermat

A mat originally made of cork and now usually of thin card, for soaking up beer spillage under glasses. Beermats are regarded by brewers as promotional material and by many customers as collectable items. The word 'tegestologist' has been coined for a collector of beermats.

## Club Room

A disappearing facility, a private room where Pigeon societies, angling clubs and RAOB (Buffs) etc. could meet in private and enjoy a drink without disturbing regular customers.

## Gill

- A quarter of a pint, most frequently used to indicate spirit measures. The 'optics' in England are generally one sixth of a gill and in Scotland one fifth of a gill
- Slang term for any drink as in 'let's go for a gill'
- Term used wrongly for a half pint of beer in Lancashire and Yorkshire

## Half

Don't ask for this in Scotland or Ireland as you will not get a half pint of beer, but instead a measure of whisk(e)y.

## Long Pull

Serving over-measure, as for example, a generous 'half' into a pint glass. This is a specific offence under the Licensing Act, whereas serving short measure is not. (It is dealt with under the weights and measures legislation).

## Mead

Alcoholic liquor of fermented honey and water.

## Parlour

The landlord's own bar room, usually a seating area behind the bar front, sometimes in the landlord's private quarters. Admission is traditionally by invitation only. Such bars are now scarce.

Locally, until recently, the Woodthorpe Hotel (Holt's) had such a 'private' drinking area where residents and a favoured few could drink. The pub has recently undergone extensive internal refurbishment, upon which the room has disappeared.

## Smoke Room

The forerunner of the lounge, especially in the North of England; originally a room where customers retired to smoke.

## Snob Screen

A pivoted decorated screen above the bar counter, designed (in Victorian pubs) to allow 'snobs' to drink in private, without being observed by their perceived social inferiors across the bar. In these more egalitarian times, snob screens remain prized features of a few pubs and are much sought after by collectors of Breweriana.

## Snug

A small room in a pub which though not specifically set aside for, were used mainly by 'unaccompanied' ladies in the days it was considered improper for them to frequent the main bar areas.

The most famous Snug in Britain was seen by millions in the TV series 'Coronation Street' where Minnie Caldwell, Ena Sharples and Martha Longhurst would sit, sipping their Milk Stouts.

Nowadays this is a rare facility as most have been 'knocked into' to enlarge the main drinking areas.

*Ena Sharples, Minnie Caldwell and Martha Longhurst in the snug of the Rovers' return in the Coronation Street TV programme ©Granada TV*

## Stillage

A wooden framework on which casks are set up in the cellar, also known as 'thralls' or 'horsing'.

## Top Up

A request to bar staff to fill the glass to the correct level so as to receive a full measure. In British law it is necessary to ask for a top up and be refused before proceeding with a complaint of short measure.

## Tap Room

Basic public bar, traditionally where customers would sit alongside the stillaged casks of beer. The back bar in the Coopers Arms in Burton-upon-Trent is one of the more famous surviving examples.

## Ullage

The word is derived from an old French one '*ouillage*' meaning the empty space in a cask from which wine is being drawn, now the licensing trades description for waste beer such as beer drawn off from pumps before serving, beer left in the casks, spillage etc. Most brewers give publicans an 'ullage allowance'. However, some unscrupulous landlords filter ullage beer, along with the contents of drip trays, back into good casks.

## Vault

North of England alternative to the Public Bar. Traditionally used for card games, dominoes and darts. Would also be used by workers in dirty clothing. Generally sparsely furnished and the beer slightly cheaper.

The vault is rapidly becoming a thing of the past as most National Brewers dispense with this facility when modernising their public houses, preferring to open them up into one roomed establishments.

Originally the Vault was the room where the casks were stored.

## Zymurgy

The art and science of brewing.

*Crown Brewery, Bury letterhead 1936*

*A History of Whitefield Pubs*

# Bay Horse           Unsworth

*Photograph A: The old Bay Horse taken around the 1940s*

When we look at the modern Bay Horse now it is hard to imagine that its history dates back almost three hundred years. One early recorded mention of the old inn is in the Manchester Mercury newspaper of the 28th January 1776 in an announcement proclaiming that the inn was to be sold by public auction, the announcement reads:

*'To be sold to the best bidder at the house of Mr Robert Stott. The sign of the Bayhorse Inn, in Unsworth, in the Parish of Prestwich, in the county of Lancaster, on the 13th February next, 1776, between the hours of one and four of the clock in the afternoon of the same day, subject to such conditions of sale as shall then and there be produced, the freehold estate of inheritance, situate, standing and being in Little Heaton, in the Parish of Prestwich, aforesaid, consisting of good housing, with seven acres of land of the Lancashire measure, in meadowing, arable and pasture ground, and now in the possession of John Dawson as tenant thereof. For further particulars enquire Jonas Lancashire and Joshiah Lancashire, the owners; or of the said John Dawson, who will shew the premises.'*

Who the 'best bidder' was at this auction is not clear. A John Jackson kept the inn before 1770 after John Dawson, although the Earl of Derby appears to have become the new owner about this time. It is likely John Jackson was a tenant of the Earl of Derby and not the purchaser.

> Unsworth Wakes used to be held twice a year outside the Bay Horse and around the Unsworth Pole, referred to locally in Lancashire dialect as the 'pow'. The Pole was presented to the village by the Earl of Derby, though nowadays no-one seems to know why. During the Wakes the Pole or 'pow' would be greased and a prize offered to anyone able to climb to the top of it. Many a jug of ale was downed at these events and no doubt many an attempt to scale the 'pow' was made afterwards!

*Photograph B: Pole Lane down the side of the pub. The signpost says 'To Heaton Park'. Unsworth Post Office can be seen to the left of the picture*

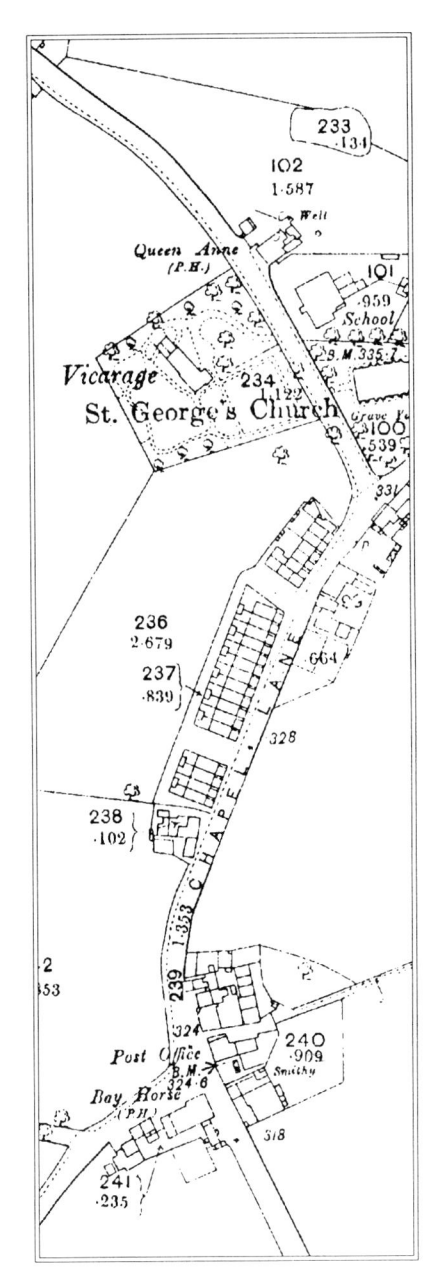

**Unsworth 1893 (O.S.)**

*Photograph C: The old inn had very low ceilings which over the years had 'accumulated' thousands of pencilled names, initials and comments.*

One story tells of a man who frequented the inn who had what was then referred to as a 'gadabout' wife who never quite managed to have his meals ready when he arrived home. One day on his way out he carried her to the mangle and wound her petticoats and skirt into the rollers as far as they would go, then took off the handle, saying that he 'thowt hoo would be theer when he coom wom at neet'.

Another tale tells of a local man who enjoyed a glass of beer or two in the Bay Horse. He decided to build himself a cart and did so in his house. He had to break it up again to get it out!

The Chief Constable's report of 1889 listed the inn as having no spare beds, facilities for feeding up to forty persons, stabling for three horses and was 440 yards (Queen Anne) and 2,340 yards (Hollins Bush) from the nearest two fully licensed public houses.

The main industry in Unsworth was handloom weaving. One local weaver, James Holt, became the father of a son born on the 25th January 1813 and named him Joseph. Joseph Holt went on to establish the Derby Brewery in Cheetham Hill in 1860 when he was aged 47. To this day Holt's excellent beers are revered throughout the land.

In 1914 his son Edward bought the Bay Horse, Joseph Holt, a native of Unsworth, had returned home.

*Unsworth Man, Joseph Holt 1813-1886*

## Origin of Name

It has long mistakenly been thought that public houses called 'Bay Horse' derived their names from the fact that there was usually a smithy nearby and carters and other horsemen would take refreshment at the inn whilst waiting for their horses to be shod (whilst the horse was in the bay). The true origin of the name Bay Horse is much more interesting and is relevant to the history of the district.

'Bay' and 'say' are two types of cloth. Bay is more familiar as 'baize' which derives from the plural of the word (French-baies). It is a coarse woollen cloth with a long nap. 'Say' (feminine of saie) is a cloth of fine texture similar to 'serge'. In Colchester, Essex, there is a public house called the 'Bay and Say'; the sign shows a man and woman in sixteenth-century costume, each carrying a bolt of cloth (roll).

The reference is to the Flemish weavers who came to settle in parts of Britain. Sir John Radcliffe brought many weavers from Flanders to the Bury and Whitefield areas in the fourteenth-century in order to improve the local weaving trade. Salford actually has a public house called the 'Flemish Weaver'.

The Bay Horse (the horse that drew the cart) would have been the mode of transport in which the bay

# A History of Whitefield Pubs

and say would have been collected from the 'cottage industry' around various villages and hamlets.

Quite naturally the village inn would have been the place where matters relating to local industry would have been discussed and no doubt the drivers of these bay horses would have called for refreshment.

It must have been a common sight to see a bay horse outside the village inn and eventually the inn became known as the Bay Horse.

Unfortunately, over the years of decline in these local cottage industries (and indeed a national decline generally in the home-spun textile industry) such terminology as 'bay' and 'say' have been lost, corrupted and even redefined. In some instances the 'bay horse' has become a 'dray horse'. The large front window in the present (new) Bay Horse public house depicts a horse drawing a cart laden with beer barrels and crates! Perhaps James Holt the Unsworth weaver and father of Joseph Holt would have had something to 'saie' on this matter.

### Known Licensees

| | |
|---|---|
| John Dawson | 1766 |
| John Jackson | late 1760s |
| Edward Royle | 1802 -1809 |
| James Brown | 1810 -1818 |
| John Hamilton | 1840s |
| James Hamilton (his son?) | 1850s |
| Thomas Lord | 20 9 1883 |
| Jane Lord | 26 8 1886 |
| Robert Hampson | 28 3 1895 |
| James Riley | 8 7 1928 |
| Ernest Jackson | 17 10 1932 |
| Fred Davenport | 4 12 1932 |
| Albert Earnest Bealson | 5 6 1935 |
| Thomas R Thomson | 18 11 1936 |
| Frederick Jackson | 2 10 1957 |
| Hilda Muriel Jackson | 11 2 1959 |
| Kathleen Madden | 2 10 1963 |
| Herbert W Redman | 6 1 1966 |
| Dorothy Redman | 9 12 1977 |
| James Wild | 6 2 1980 |
| Kenneth Coleman | 13 4 1988 |
| Joanne Lesley Fallone | 4 12 1991 |

By the late 1950s Unsworth was growing fast with the arrival of the new housing estates and Holt's Brewery decided that a larger and more modern public house was required. In 1960 the demolition of the old inn and the building of the new got underway.

Fortunately for us, a local man, Frank Williams, was around with his cine camera as the pub was demolished and filmed it. With the aid of a computer, we have been able to capture stills of the film. They are shown below and on the following page.

**Photograph D: A demolition man starts to strip the roof slates of the apex**

**Photograph E: Then down it goes**

**Photograph F: Next goes the right side front wall...**

*A History of Whitefield Pubs*

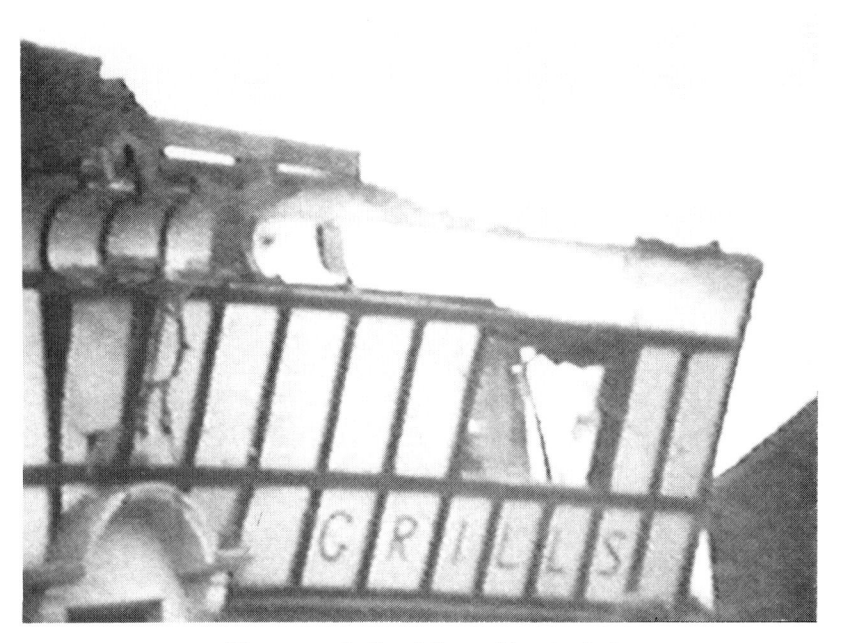

*Photograph G: ..followed by the left*

*Photograph H: After the demolition work starts on the present pub*

*Photograph I: Next ... The large front lounge window is fitted. Unfortunately shortly afterwards this window was smashed. The present window being an identical replacement (depicting the Horse and Cart)*

*Photograph J: Lightfoot the glaziers installing the Pole Lane side windows*

*Photograph K: The modern bay horse, built in 1962*

*Photograph L: The most recent Bay Horse sign (1993)*

Bloodgood and Santini, in their 'Horseman's directory' define 'bay' as horse colour ranging from light brown to rich mahogany, but always with black points (ie main and tail) which distinguishes it from any variety of chestnut. (At Astley Bridge near Bolton there is a 'Bay Mare' public house). Technically a female horse is only a mare if it has reached the age of five (thoroughbred) or four other breeds or after it has been bred to a stallion.

The present day Bay Horse (above) is built on the same site as its predecessor which in turn replaced an earlier inn. Once within the 'Pilkington' boundary, its history may well date back to the days when Unsworth was known as Houndsworth.

Robert Hampson, who was landlord from 1895 until 1928, was convicted on the 21st of November 1912 for selling adulterated whisky! He was fined ten shillings plus costs, which came to a total of two pounds, two shillings and sevenpence.

Page 27

*A History of Whitefield Pubs*

# Brown Mare                                        Higher Lane

The first mention of Whitefield's 'Brown Mare' appears in Baines' Directory for 1838. It is listed again in the Post Office Directory for 1843 with Joseph Gawkrodger as victualler (see extract). Another directory for 1850 lists Jacob Greaves as victualler. The same Jacob Greaves later registers as the keeper of the Bay Horse, Higher Lane in 1858, with his wife Susannah taking over from him in 1861. A census return for number 69, Higher Lane (the Brown Mare site) for 1881 lists John Howarth (aged 72), brewer and James Greaves aged 30 (Jacob's son) as assistant brewer. On the 29th May 1881 James Greaves also became the licensee at the 'General Jackson' (later, the Albert) on Oak Lane. The Brown Mare was demolished around 1885.

The Brown Mare was located in between No. 67 Higher Lane and the 'Broxups'. Both these properties are still standing. The actual piece of ground the old inn stood on is now part of a garden that fronts a modern bungalow. There is not the slightest visual evidence that one of the town's oldest and grandest hostelries ever existed there.

*Artist's impression of one of Whitefield's oldest and grandest hostelries*

Fray James, coal dealer, Cinder hill, Outwood
FREE GRAMMAR SCHOOL, Stand—Rev. Robt. Thompson Miniss, head master ; Jas. Smethurst, writing master
FREE SCHOOL, Ringley—John Barnsdall, jun. master
Gawkrodger Jos. vict. *Brown Mare*, Higher la. Whitefield
Gerrard George, manager, Mill lane, Radcliffe bridge
Gill Robert O. Esq. Sedgley
Gooden Thomas, shopkeeper, Radcliffe hall

*Extract from Post Office directory of 1843*

*This was once the gateway to the Brown Mare*

> It is often only through old recognizances, directories and census returns that we are able to ascertain the existence of inns and beerhouses such as the Brown Mare. Even if they are long extinct, often not even to be photographed, we can keep them alive.
>
> Sometimes, even the Licensing Registers are hard to obtain. Only in the last month, a number of previously unseen registers have surfaced in Manchester, having been misplaced for several years. Without those registers, we would be without the names of at least twenty licensees.

# Beehive Inn

## Bury New Road

The most probable explanation of how the Beehive pub got its name is the fact that in the early 1800s and onwards the Besses o'th' Barn area had many beekeepers, most of them registered as such in local directories. The beehive has long been a sign of industry. In many cases it simply appeared as a sign because of its distinctive shape.

In the 1840s Messrs. George Fletcher and Company erected a factory in Unsworth for the purpose of weaving nankeens and fancy drills. It was owned by a Mr Fitton and called the 'Beehive Spindle Works'. Although Unsworth was part of Pilkington in those days, a connection between the pub and the factory cannot be substantiated.

*Photograph A shows the Besses Boy's Band passing the Bee Hive after returning home triumphant from Belle Vue as British Champions in 1946. The band won the title in 1945, 1946 and 1947. In 1948 all other bands refused to enter unless the Besses Band withdrew; this they refused to do and the competition did not take place. They won again in 1949 and 1950 (These competitions were sponsored by the Daily Herald).*

**Photograph A: The Besses Boy's Band return triumphant in 1946**

Historically the title deeds show that as distant as 1812 the land was owned by a Mr Joseph Scholes and a Mr Charles Patefield. Joseph Scholes is listed in early directories as a grocer and corn dealer residing at Stone Pale. Scholes' grocers have long been associated with the town and, until quite recent times had a shop opposite the Beehive. Photograph B was taken from there in 1942. The lady in the doorway is Ruth Galloway, now Ruth Cocken who still lives in Whitefield.

**Photograph B: The Beehive in 1942.
The attached shop on the right was to be removed later**

We know that as late as 1831 the site of the Beehive was still building land. The first mention of the site as an inn comes from the Rate register (Bury Archives) for 1864 where the premises are described thus:

*Beer-House, Brewhouse and Cellar, Rateable value £16-12s-2d*

so we know that it brewed its own beer then. Whether the Beehive brewhouse supplied any other public houses in the area is a matter of speculation. Research on this matter has found no evidence that it did, so we must assume it was simply a 'home brew pub' until bought by the Crown brewery in 1885 when it would have been supplied by them. Nowadays the Beehive brewhouse is used as a bottle store.

The first owner that there is a record of was Richard Hilton and he sold it to E Mills and John Mills (John lived at 12 Bolton Road, Elton) in the 1880s. From the deeds there is an assignment dated the 27th January 1885 when a Mr E Mills with others assigned to the Crown Brewing Company of Bury, the land with the inn, shop and cottages erected thereon.

*A History of Whitefield Pubs*

Dutton's Blackburn Brewery Ltd (founded 1799 by Thomas Dutton) bought 744 square yards of land with the Beehive on site from the Crown Brewing Company of Bury on the 22nd March 1960. Dutton's in turn were taken over by Whitbread in 1964 who have retained ownership.

More recently, in 1957 some major alterations took place at the Beehive. They included the off-sales department with its access on Victoria Lane being dispensed with. The cellar access via a trap door staircase behind the bar was re-sited where the out sales had been and a window put in the gable end to provide daylight onto the new staircase. The biggest job was the removal of the shop which was attached to the right-hand side of the building. This was demolished and a new gable end built. Revolving doors were installed at the main entrance at the same time.

The barrel drop was bricked up and a new, more easily accessible one was made on Victoria Lane (formally Narrow Lane). The old steel 'bull-ring' used by the dray men for lowering barrels by rope is still in the wall opposite the old drop. (In the old days it was quite common for beer to be delivered in wooden 'Hogsheads'; these were 54 gallon barrels that weighed around 149 lbs empty. Nowadays the aluminium and stainless steel 36 gallon barrels are in general use and are much lighter).

What is now the vault (or tap room) at the far end of the bar on the left as you walk in, was used for many years as the licensee's private quarters before they were moved upstairs.

A section of this wall has now been removed enabling vault customers to be served from the main bar. The room on the left as you enter from Bury New Road was the original vault and the room to the right, the lounge. Since then the pub has been 'opened up' with the removal of the internal walls.

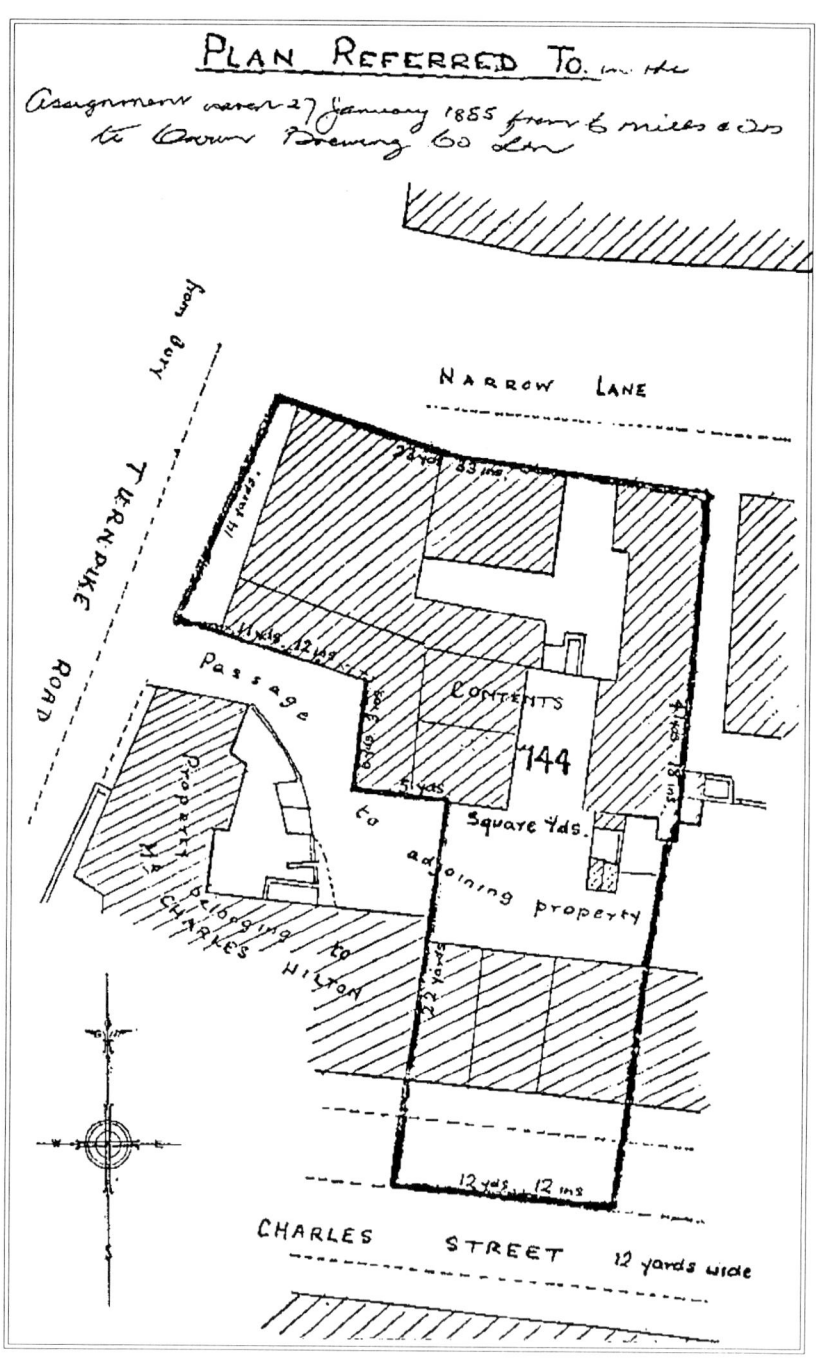

*1885 Plan of the Beehive's location*

More alterations and improvements were made in 1986 and took twelve weeks to complete. This work commenced on the 18th August and consisted of the removal of the revolving doors which by now had been considered a fire hazard in that they could restrict the rapid exit by a number of people. The old glass roof that covered the passage to the toilets was replaced with a flat asphalt roof and a new toilet block was built. The Beehive window that was removed from the passage wall is now re-sited and clearly visible in the wall that separates the lounge from the pool room. The pool room used to be the music room with a piano. When Annie Wheeler was landlady there was a one armed pianist who used to play there by the name of John Emmerson.

A second identical window was removed from the premises by the brewery, possibly for use elsewhere.

The old single stable with its cobbled floor and hay manger was demolished, having been badly fire damaged sometime in the 1940s. The old Coach House on Victoria Lane

**Photograph C: A rare sight these days**

**Photograph E: Dutton's OBJ**

**Photograph F: Dutton's Special**

had its old wooden doors removed and replaced with an up and over door for its present use as a garage. (In the 1950s a local motor cycle club used the coach house as a meeting place and repaired their machines there).

In the lounge the chimney breast was opened up and a coal effect gas fire was fitted.

Photograph C shows a section of the tiled wall in what had been the out sales (now top of cellar steps) with a superb and rare Crown Brewery Company logo still surviving. Sadly it is not visible from the public areas.

> The buildings of the old Crown Brewery in Bury (founded 1870) have now completely vanished. The ASDA Supermarket was built on the site (now Kwik Save). The associated 'Crown Hotel' still stands on the corner of Heywood Street and Rochdale Road.

Sometime in 1981 a vandal smashed the original Beehive acid etched window in the vault from Victoria Lane. This was replaced with ordinary frosted glass. More recently whilst 'bottling up' Mr Yarwood found the old Crown Brewery sign that had originally been fixed to the wall next to the front door. (It can be seen on photographs A and B). John Hannan, the present landlord has had it restored by David Mills, a local sign writer and it is now proudly displayed on a wall in the public bar area.

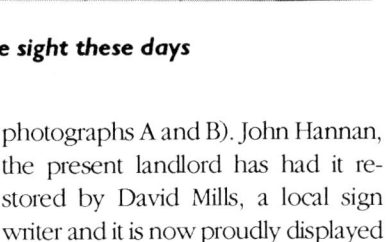

Photograph D below shows the Besses Boys Band, now some distance from the Beehive on the same procession as photograph A.

**Photograph D: Taken on the same day as photograph A in 1946**

# A History of Whitefield Pubs

Photographs E and F are of a 1960s Dutton's beer mat, showing both sides, OBJ - 'Oh Be Joyful' and 'Special Bitter'. When Whitbread took over Dutton's in 1964, Dutton's beer lovers were not very 'joyful' and changed their version of OBJ to 'Oh be Jesus' (pronounced with an Irish accent).

*Photograph G: The 'Hive' sign 1992*

Since the 1860s the Beehive has had twenty-three known licensees. The longest serving so far was Thomas Henry Howard, with 21 years (1956-1977). Next is Annie Wheeler with 18 years (1937 - 1955). John Hannan, the present tenant is currently the third longest serving, in his fourteenth year of tenure.

*Photograph H: Beehive outing, 1930*

The picture above records a 1930s coach trip from the Beehive. It is not yet known where they were going, but somewhere in the picture are William Bradwell, messrs. Thorpe, Berry, Hill, Garbutt, Hardman, Hilton and Nally. If you can recognise anyone else please contact the author or publisher.

Both front windows were smashed recently and have now been duplicated and reinstalled.

*Photograph I: Replacement window*

Photograph J was taken in the early 1960s just after the change from Dutton's to Whitbread. The Coach House can be seen to the left of the picture. Notice also the much wider pavement than nowadays, and the lamp post, not on the earlier photographs.

*Photograph J: In the 1960s*

Another former Dutton's pub, also called the Beehive in Penrith had the following inscription on its sign: In this hive we are all alive. Good liquors make us funny, if you be dry step in and try the virtue of our honey

### Known Licensees

| Richard Hilton | 1860s |
|---|---|
| Sarah Hilton | 12 1 1874 |
| George Wardle | 1 6 1877 |
| Benjamin Webster | 25 5 1878 |
| Richard Howarth | 28 5 1885 |
| John Wild | 21 1 1886 |
| Walter Kirkman | 11 11 1886 |
| Joseph Hartley | 19 1 1888 |
| Thomas Entwistle | 23 2 1888 |
| Alice Entwistle | 8 12 1892 |
| Thomas Jones | 11 1 1894 |
| Samuel Fogg | 3 12 1900 |
| Thomas Jones | 18 5 1905 |
| John Dickinson | 24 7 1911 |
| Sarah E Dickinson | 15 7 1918 |
| John Dickinson | 12 2 1920 |
| Fred Farrar | 8 2 1923 |
| William Hilton | 1 12 1932 |
| Annie Wheeler | 8 3 1937 |
| John Craig | 3 3 1955 |
| Thomas H Howard | 16 4 1956 |
| Rus Gibbon | 17 4 1977 |
| John L Hannan | 11 6 1980 |

*The Beehive 1992, 50 years on from Photograph B with the shop now gone. Notice that the arched fanlight above the door has been squared off and the old roof boards have been removed.*

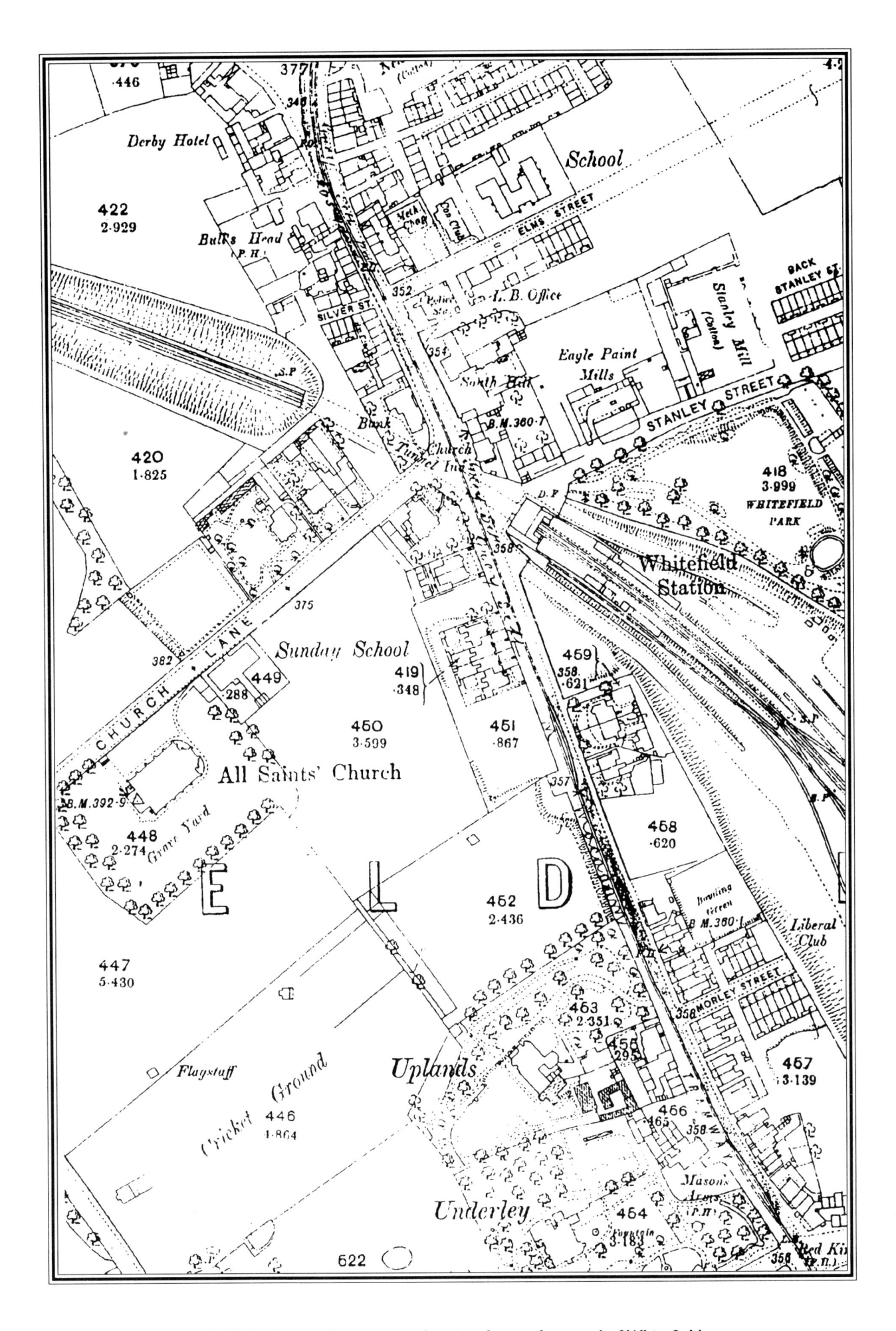

*1893 Ordnance Survey map showing the northern end of Whitefield*

# Coach & Horses and Bentley Brewery, Kirkhams

*A 'Charabanc' Outing from the Coach (circa 1912)*

The Coach and Horses was built in 1830 and in those early days was used as a staging post for the Burnley to Manchester mail coach. It also served as a stop for the normal daily omnibus service between Manchester and Bury where the guard would give a blast on his horn on approach. Hence the pub's name.

The Coach and Horses was owned for many years by Robert Bentley who also founded the Brewery there. As well as supplying his own house he also supplied beer to several other Prestwich and Whitefield public houses including the Cross Keys, Lily Hill Street, the Black Horse, Bury New Road and the Plough Inn, Rainsough.

In 1879 the Bentley family sold out to Gustavus F Carrington. The Coach and Horses and the Brewery were run by his sons with Leo A Carrington taking charge of the pub, with Alfred and Gustavus Ernest Carrington taking charge of the brewing operation and trading as GF Carrington and Sons, Bentley Brewery.

Extracts from the deeds for the Coach and Horses up to this point read as follows:

*October 1873* (Copy of lease)
*Joseph Bentley leased the property from the Earl of Derby, June 1876. Assignment via a mortgage - Joseph Bentley to Martha Openshaw and others.*
*December 9th 1879. Trustees of JF Bentley to Gustavus F Carrington of Jersey, a ship owner.*
*January 21st 1896. Assignment of the Prestwich Brewery (with steam engine) and the Coach and Horses to Alfred Carrington and Gustavus Ernest Carrington, Brewers, late GF Carrington.*

GF Carrington's Will mentions four other properties in his estate. They were

- The Royal Oak Beerhouse 30/32 Upper Duke Street, Hulme
- Mona Arms Beerhouse, 79 Upper Duke Street, Hulme
- Queens Arms, 27 Birch Street, Hulme
- Cambridge Hotel, Regent Road, Salford and the Monarch Brewery

The original iron bridge at Besses o'th' Barn was known as Bentley Bridge (also known locally as the 'Cephos' Bridge because of the Cephos advert painted on it).

> A note of interest here is the fact that in later years when the tram tracks were laid, only open top double deckers came down Bury Old Road from Besses junction. The roofed double deckers went down Bury New Road to Prestwich and beyond, but these were just too high to pass under Bentley Bridge.
>
> Some time around 1915 one did go down the Old Road by mistake and hit the bridge, causing serious injury to some top deck passengers.

In 1897 the Carringtons decided to sell up and an auction was held at the Thatched House Hotel on Market Street, in Manchester on the 27th July.

From the deeds we learn that at this auction all the above properties were purchased by John Henry Davies. He is described as an Estate Agent but was also active in the brewing businesses of the Manchester Brewery Company and later Walker & Homfray Ltd (who eventually merged with Wilsons Brewery in 1949).

On the 16th December 1897 Davies sold land and the Coach and Horses lease to Edward Holt (son of Joseph Holt, the founder of Holt's Brewery). Davies had formally acquired the pub and brewery by assignments dated the 1st and 2nd November 1897. In view of this very short time span between purchase and disposal it must be assumed that Holts had an agreement with Davies to buy the Coach and Horses at the time of the auction.

Technically, the Coach and Horses would have been a Manchester Brewery Co House for a matter of forty-four days; it is possible, however that Davies at the time of the auction was acting as a broker rather than in his capacity as a Director of the firm. If this was the case, then the Coach and Horses was never a Manchester Brewery House.

Davies retained the Bentley Brewery which was closed down shortly afterwards. It is almost certain that the modern brewing equipment was transferred to the Manchester Brewery's premises, the Britannia Brewery on Brodie Street, Manchester.

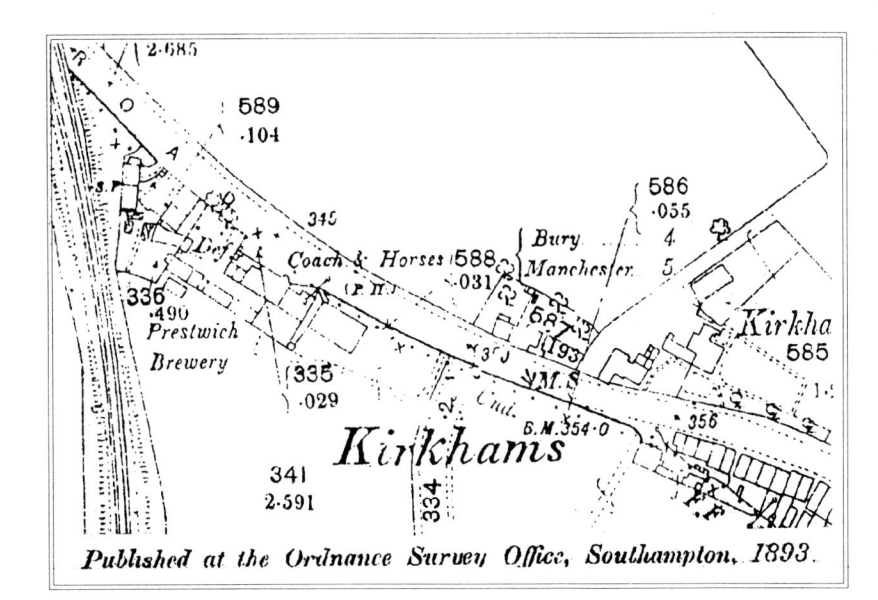

**Photograph B: The Coach and Horses in 1990. It was once a buffalo**

At the auction the properties were described as follows:

*'Land on the southerly side of Bury Old Road, Prestwich, containing 3,377 superficial square yards or thereabouts, with a frontage of 110 yards 3 inches together with the public house known as the Coach and Horses and the outbuildings erected thereon'.*

The Brewery was described as *'A steam brewery, better known as Prestwich Brewery. The premises and plant are modern and comprise store cellars, working cellars, rack room, store room, engine and boiler house, malt room, hop room, cooling house, fully equipped with machinery and plant for brewing'.*

On the 22nd December 1926 Joseph Holt Ltd bought the lease from the Earl of Derby estate.

From the 1940s to 1980 the Coach and Horses was kept by the Bentley family and it is purely coincidental that the original owners were also Bentleys. The two families are unrelated and there were fourteen licensees and sixty-five years between them.

### Known Licensees

| | |
|---|---|
| Robert Bentley | 1830 |
| Joseph Bentley | 1872 |
| Leo A Carrington | 23 10 1879 |
| Charles Smith | 21 6 1883 |
| FN & Mary Thornley | 17 3 1886 |
| Edward Philips | 10 3 1887 |
| CJ Nolan | 16 6 1887 |
| Matilda Wardle | 26 4 1888 |
| Alice Grievson | 6 12 1894 |
| J & Sarah Sheperd | 14 6 1900 |
| Wright Barlow | 14 11 1901 |
| Albert H Brown | July 1903 |
| William H Richardson | 12 9 1909 |
| George Harrison | 8 9 1910 |
| J Warburton | 6 12 1917 |
| Samuel Creswell | 9 12 1927 |
| Charles Randolf Bentley | 9 2 1944 |
| Robert Hamer Bentley | 2 10 1951 |
| Zena Bentley | 1980 |
| Arthur Daniel Burnham | 3 9 1980 |

The first Bentley family kept the pub for nearly 50 years and the Bentley's of more recent times for almost 40 years. No wonder that with almost 90 years of Bentley association with the Coach and Horses, it has been mistakenly thought that they were the same family.

**Extract from 1893 Ordnance Survey Map**

*A History of Whitefield Pubs*

**Photograph C: Charles Randolf Bentley, Landlord 1944-1951**

Bob Bentley was a qualified butcher and had his own shop before he went in the army. Later he helped his father run the Brunswick pub on Union Street (now Riverside) Lower Broughton, and the Wagon and Horses at Irlam o'th' Heights before taking over the Coach and Horses from his father.

Bob Bentley died in 1980 and his wife Zena continued to run the pub with the help of her two sons,

**Photograph D: Bob and Zena in the back garden at the rear of the Coach**

John and Ronnie until September 1980 when the present landlord, Arthur Burnham, took over. Sadly, Zena died in 1988.

> Many a discussion and argument has taken place over whether the Coach and Horses is in Prestwich or Whitefield since it stands on the Urban District boundary between the two. Technically it is in both, as for postal services it is in Whitefield and for electoral purposes it is in Prestwich. For historical reasons, it is in this book!

**Photograph E: Jim Clayton, a 1930s regular (shown here in his younger days)**

Jim Clayton (shown above) was a regular at the Coach and Horses in the 1920s and 30s. One day Jim was in the pub having a pint when Sam Creswell the landlord at the time had found a leg of lamb in the vault and nobody had claimed it. Sam, knowing that Jim had ten children, gave it to him.

May Barker who is now 74 and one of Jim's daughters recalls *'When dad came home with that leg of lamb we thought it was Christmas and mother put it in the oven straight away'*. Next door to the Claytons lived a widow who was courting an Irishman and later his raised voice could be heard in the street telling people his leg of lamb had been stolen. The truth was, that after a few pints he had forgotten

**Photograph F: Robert (Bob) Bentley, Landlord 1951-1980**

**Photograph G: Ronnie, Zena and John (inset) behind the Coach bar**

where he had left it. It seems he retraced his steps round the pubs he had visited, but Sam, realising maybe he should have hung on to it a bit longer, denied all knowledge of ever having seen it. May recalls, *'You can imagine the panic in our house. This man in the street now shouting about his leg of lamb and the smell of cooking meat in mum's oven drifting into the street'.*

However, the lamb was thoroughly enjoyed by the Claytons and nobody was any the wiser - until now!

In researching a pub's history the search for information can often unearth sad and tragic events. The following did just that. Below is an extract taken from the Prestwich and Whitefield Guide, Friday October 19th 1928.

> **Death of a well known Whitefield resident**
>
> *Much sympathy has been expressed in the district with the family of Mr. Nelson Burdaky of Malverna, Bury Old Road, Whitefield, who was accidentally killed last Thursday, October 11th, whilst crossing the road at Kirkhams. He was secretary of the RAOB Lodge which meets at the Coach and Horses Hotel. He had been on business at the Hotel and although the motor lorry driver sounded his horn and applied both his brakes, Mr. Burdaky went forward and was struck in the back, the near side wheel going over the upper part of the body. Mr. Burdaky was keenly interested in the work of the RAOB (Buffs) and had worked very hard in its cause and he will be greatly missed.*

The inquest was held at Whitefield Conservative Club on Friday October 12th 1928 and a report appeared in the Bury Times on Saturday October 13th 1928. (The Coroner's report from that edition is held on microfilm at Bury Reference Library). Mr. Burdaky was 58 when he was killed. The photograph shown was taken some years earlier.

***Photograph H: Nelson Burdaky killed outside the Coach 1928***

Joe Mason was also a regular at the Coach and Horses in Sam Creswell's days and was a very inventive man. He used to mint his own half-crowns on a cast mould.

His raw materials consisted of knifes, forks and spoons or anything else he could get his hands on. These he would melt down in his kitchen. Apparently he wasn't such a villain for he is remembered for treating all the kids in the neighbourhood to bags of sweets, usually half a crown's worth at a time!

He was once arrested whilst sitting on the doorstep of the Coach enjoying a pint. It seems Sam had got suspicious. However, as he was being taken to the police station he slipped the remainder of his half crowns into the policeman's pocket and on being searched was found to have none of the illegal coins on his person and was released. But alas, Joe continued passing over his counterfeit coins and was arrested again at a later date. The result was Joe had nine months off the beer!

## Of More Recent Times

In 1986 the tranquillity of the Coach was interrupted by a huge explosion outside the front of the pub, which blew in some of the vault windows. The force of the blast was so great it also blew in the hardware shop window on the opposite side of the road.

The cause, a heater fuelled by a propane gas cylinder, had been left burning in the back of a customer's van on the car park and unventilated the cylinder had exploded, setting fire to the by now buckled van. The van was on the car park between the pub and Kirkhams Garage, where thousands of gallons of petrol lay in the tanks only a few feet away. The blazing van and surrounding area was doused with thousands of gallons of foam by the Fire Brigade. It is probably only a coincidence but the owner of the van stopped calling in shortly afterwards!

1990 saw the floor behind the bar which was in danger of collapsing, removed and replaced with new timbers. Whilst this work was in

***Photograph I: May Barker (vivid recollections of leg of lamb)***

# A History of Whitefield Pubs

*Photograph J: The old crooked bottle shelves that seemed to defy gravity were the subject of much discussion among the locals*

### Kirkhams

*Kirkhams area gets its name from Thomas Kirkham, a cotton merchant who was also a warden of Prestwich Church. In 1773 he had a house built which was a plain three storeyed building surrounded by a high wall and named it Kirkhams House. It stood on the corner of what is now Derby Road (then farmland) approximately where the Chinese chip shop stands today. The last tenant was a Mr Lamb, a local farmer who eventually sold the house with land for building purposes.*

progress a temporary bar was built in the snug which had its floor renewed some weeks earlier. One customer had joked '*If that floor isn't replaced soon, we'll need taller bar staff!*'

Below: Bob Bentley organised many 'Coach' trips over the years. This particular one was to Morecambe in the early 1960s. On the homeward journey Bob sat front right.

*Photograph K: Temporary bar in the snug*

*Photographs M (above) and N (below): Coach trip to Morecambe*

*Photograph L: Snug minus the floor*

Page 38

*A History of Whitefield Pubs*

# Church Inn                                    Bury New Road

Stand Church was completed in 1826 and the Church Inn, built around 1830 was named after it. The horse buses pulled up there every hour on their way to Besses junction and to Bury. There were two per day on Sundays, Mondays, Wednesdays and Thursdays and one per day on Tuesdays, Fridays and Saturdays.

The first owner was Samuel Mather who was probably the father of James Mather, the landlord, who was there for over 30 years. He was apparently a man of substance for he had a large family and his children were all well educated. Some were distinguished for their musical talent and some went into the teaching profession. In later years one of his sons, James, became the first Mayor of Eccles and another, Francis, was the proprietor of Whitefield Mill.

> One of Samuel Mather's daughters married a Frenchman and locals at the inn were astonished one afternoon on the arrival of the 'bus' when six large trunks were handed down, each one bearing the name 'Charles Ferdinand Desiree Alex Delener'. He also brought with him his dog called 'Nero' and used to amuse the customers by opening the bay window and throwing a stick out across the road into a field on the other side. Nero would leap out of the window and quickly retrieve it. (The road was very narrow those days).

At the gable end of the inn was a superb Jargonelle pear tree which was always well laden and the long garden reached down to Cow Lane (now Stanley Road).

When the railway came in 1879 the name was quickly altered to the 'Church Inn & Railway Hotel'. Photograph A shows landlord Robert Merrith and his wife Sarah in the doorway of the newly named Inn sometime between 1886 and 1894

**Photograph A: Robert Merrith and his wife (tenants 1886 - 1894)**

and is believed to be the only surviving photograph of the inn showing the famous pear tree.

The Chief Constable's report of 1889 describes the Church Inn as having two spare beds, facilities for feeding up to 60 persons, stabling facilities for six horses and 420 yards (Mason's Arms) and 136 yards (Wheatsheaf) from the two nearest fully licensed houses.

James Martin was the next licensee. He took over in July 1894 and his name can be seen on the skyboards on photograph B.

By now the steam tramway had arrived and this particular picture shows a Wilkinson-built standard gauge (4ft 8½ inch) locomotive No. 41 and a Starbuck-built car outside the inn. Note the destinations painted on the car's rocker panels (Bury-Whitefield). This locomotive was originally numbered 38 but was damaged by a boiler explosion in the Bury depot in 1898. After it was rebuilt it was returned to service renumbered 41 as shown here.

It would be quite natural to assume, from comparing photographs, that the Church Inn has been rebuilt

**Photograph B: Typical scene outside the Church Inn around 1894**

*A History of Whitefield Pubs*

but this is not strictly true. Although the front has changed beyond recognition, observations of the rear of the building reveal the original 1830s brickwork which is clearly visible from the bus station.

The new frontage and extension into what was the garden, along with the internal refit were carried out between 1894 and 1905. At the same time the name reverted back to the original title of Church Inn.

Note the chimney on photograph B just to the left of J Martin's name and note also the same chimney on photograph C which also clearly shows the unsymmetrical extension, often described as 'the bit stuck on the side'. The pear tree would have stood approximately where the doorway from the bar area leads into the extension.

In 1908 the inn became part of the Joseph Holt estate. Part of the contract to purchase reads: *'Land on the easterly side of Bury New Road, Whitefield, containing 838 superficial square yards or thereabouts, with a frontage of 29 yards 1 inch, together with the public house known as the Church Inn and outbuildings erected thereon'*. Purchaser - Edward Holt.

In 1925 Holt's bought the lease on the land from the Earl of Derby Estate.

***Photograph C: Unsymmetrical extension (photo 1991)***

***Photograph D: The attached stables pulled down in 1987 (photo early 1960s) Note the stables on photograph A***

***Photograph E: In 1916 the Bury-Manchester rail line was electrified. This speeded up the complete journey from 32 minutes to 24 minutes.***

Photograph D taken in the early 1960s shows the stables attached to the inn. Years ago they were rented to Watson & Stark, a firm of carriers who were based in Ramsbottom. They were only demolished as recently as the beginning of 1987.

It can be seen that the front of the building has been cleaned since this particular photograph was taken. It is thought the chap in the doorway of photograph D is Jesse Howarth, licensee 1957-1967. Also shown is the old Whitefield Railway Station (circa 1929). It had a significant bearing on the history of the Church Inn.

**Photograph F: Controversial Bill Imms**

Bill Imms was probably Whitefield's most controversial publican, but he was also a very popular one.

Originally from Liverpool, he was a professional soldier until he took over the Church Inn in 1968, retiring from the army as a Royal Artillery Sergeant

His 'main aim' was to run a typically British pub without such things as a juke box and fruit machines and would not serve anyone he overheard using offensive language. During one period there were several attacks on the pub when windows were smashed by stones. Bill claimed he was being victimised because he had refused to serve 'loud mouthed drunks and louts'. He once stood as an Independent candidate in a strong Labour ward of the town and nearly won the seat.

He was a fierce supporter of the death penalty and many a heated discussion took place across the bar. He refused to sell French wine and would not open his pub one New Year's Eve in protest over Britain joining the Common Market.

His high point of controversy came when he refused to serve a woman teacher with a pint and told another woman drinker that *'drinking beer made women fat and ugly'*. That landed him in Court in a case brought under the Sex Discrimination Act. The case attracted national press coverage, but Bill lost the case and had to agree to serve women with pints if requested. He told reporters at the time he was considering putting a penny on a pint to cover the cost of the Court case. He retired from the pub in 1968 and died four years later at the age of 68. Gone, but not forgotten!

Today women are very much part of the pub scene. The attitude to women in pubs has varied down the centuries. In Victorian times the pub was a man's stronghold; respectable women at best would probably only use the snug.

> *This was not always the case. Thomas Platter in his 'Travels in England' written in 1599 states*
>
> *'What is particularly curious is that the women as well as the men, in fact more often than they, will frequent the Taverns and Ale Houses for enjoyment. They count it a great honour to be taken there and given wine with sugar to drink! And if only one woman is invited, then she will bring three or four other women along and they will gaily toast each other; the husband afterwards thanks him who has given his wife such pleasure, for they deem it a great kindness.'*

In recent years, the provision of improved amenities to be found in pubs has to a large extent been influenced by women.

**Photograph G: Acid etched window (some were broken)**

**Photograph H: How times have changed Coronation St TV programme ©Granada Television**

Page 41

# A History of Whitefield Pubs

**Photograph I:** *The old and the new bricks (NB Whitefield Bus Station [right] opened on 3rd November 1931)*

Photograph I above shows the rear of the Church Inn clearly showing the original 1830s brickwork, with the later extensions which included the new frontage and perimeter wall in more modern brick. Notice also the chimney, centre of the picture. The original has been dropped to gutter level and also rebuilt in the newer brick.

## Known Licensees

| | |
|---|---|
| James Mather (early) | 1830s |
| John Davison | 1860s |
| Thomas Rothwell | 4 9 1876 |
| Robert Merrith | 27 5 1886 |
| James Martin | 2 7 1894 |
| Alice Ann Martin | 27 7 1905 |
| Barbara H Taylor | 2 10 1909 |
| James William Sykes | 21 7 1913 |
| James Arthur Hall | 8 1 1923 |
| Annie Hibbert | 2 2 1925 |
| William Lees | 5 6 1930 |
| Frederick Dixon | 7 2 1933 |
| John Edward Smith | 3 6 1954 |
| John Scotson | 6 9 1956 |
| Jesse Howarth | 5 12 1957 |
| Marjorie Howarth | 17 7 1967 |
| William Imms | 5 12 1968 |
| Michael W Doherty | 16 8 1978 |
| Norma Doherty | 11 7 1979 |
| Paul Anthony Naylor | 24 4 1991 |
| Brian Pearson | 8 9 1993 |

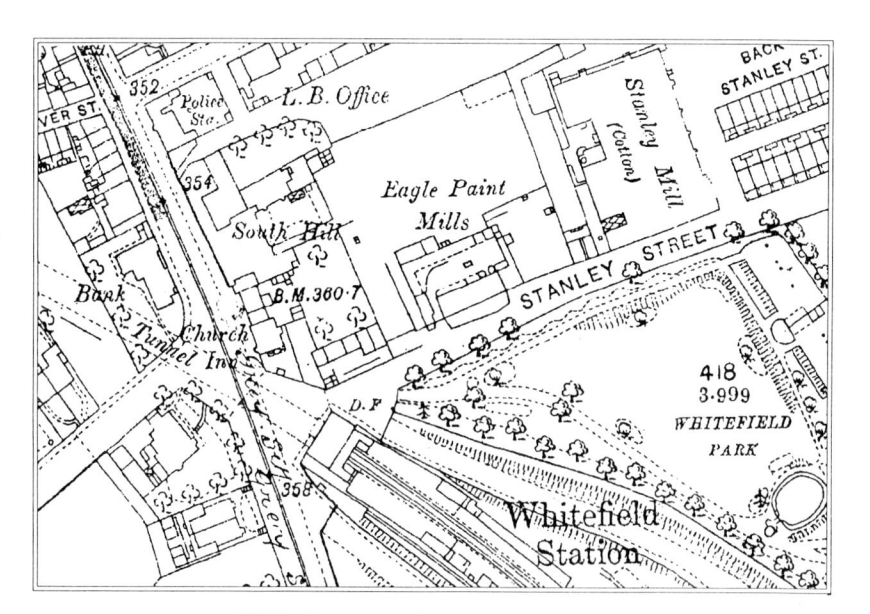

*1893 Ordnance Survey map extract*

**Photograph J:** *The Church Inn with its new signs, fitted Autumn 1991*

Page 42

# Cross Keys — Lily Hill Street

*Photograph A: When it sold Walker and Homfray's Ale*

The Cross Keys was a beerhouse from as early as 1833 when it was owned and kept by James Butterworth. The beer was supplied from the newly founded Bentley Brewery at Kirkhams. In those days it would have been a main road beerhouse, as before the later section of Bury New Road (now Manchester Road) was completed in the early 1830s and Radcliffe New Road made 1860, it stood on the old road to Bury (now Lily Hill Street) which passed by and on through the hamlet of Lily Hill.

In 1876 a public auction was held at the Church Inn, Whitefield and the Cross Keys was bought by Joseph Bentley of Bentley Brewery. Joseph died shortly afterwards and in 1879 his widow Ann Bentley sold the Cross Keys along with the Coach and Horses and attached Brewery to GF Carrington and Sons who continued to supply the beer.

The Cross Keys remained a beerhouse up until 1884 when a full Public House licence was granted. In 1897 the Carringtons disposed of all their public houses, most of which were acquired by The Manchester Brewery Company.

They were taken over by Walker & Homfrays of the Woodside Brewery, Eccles New Road, Salford in 1912, who in turn merged with Wilsons in 1949. Following the amalgamation with Walker & Homfrays the company was styled Wilson & Walker Breweries. In 1952 the Woodside Brewery, Salford, closed down and the name reverted to Wilsons Brewery.

Wilsons Newton Heath Brewery no longer exists as Wilsons are now part of the Webster's organisation. The beer is brewed and delivered from Halifax in Yorkshire.

Photograph A was taken on 2nd September 1951 and shows the pub with its Walker and Homfrays signs. Note also the word 'Inn' on the lamp over the front door.

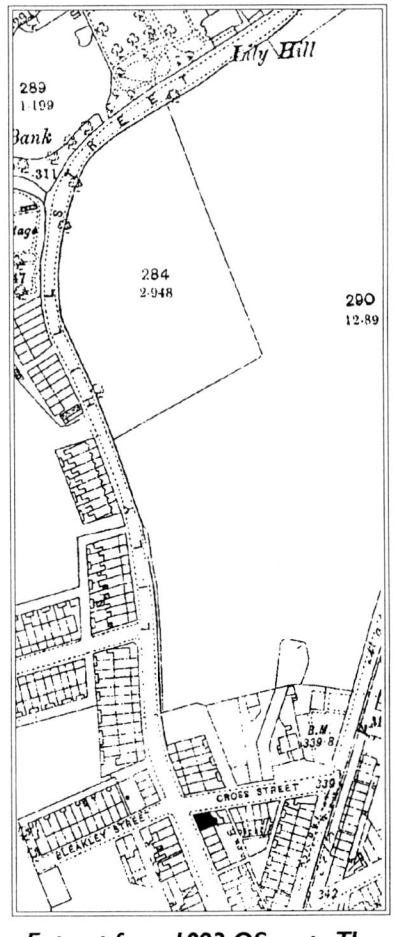

*Extract from 1893 OS map. The Cross keys is filled black*

Photograph B was taken on 7th July 1961. Notice the additional window that has appeared above the front door and the then new Whitefield Fire Station can be seen at the far end of Cross Street.

> *Cross Street appropriately runs to the side of the pub but there is no connection with this and its name. Inn signs go back many hundreds of years and the Cross Keys has always been a popular one.*
>
> *It became the emblem of St. Peter, a disciple, who Jesus named the 'Rock' and said 'Upon this rock I will build my Church and I will give thee the keys of the Kingdom of Heaven'. After the Reformation, Henry VIII decreed that any Cross Keys should be changed to the Kings Head, but a lot of them got overlooked and survive to this day.*

Photograph C shows the Cross Keys in 1952 just after the sign boards were changed to 'Fine Wilsons Ales'. The Wilsons 'Draught Board' plaque has appeared to the right of the door. Notice also that the lamp shade has gone.

A point of interest here is that before the internal alterations were

**Photograph B: July 1961 (notice the window above the door)**

**Photograph C: 1952 The signs are changed to 'Wilsons'**

**This Ken Greenhalgh painting of the Cross Keys is looking towards Lily Hill Street along Cross Street from Bury New Road.**

carried out some years ago the taproom used to be on the right as you went through the front door. The bar parlour was on the left. The original acid etched windows are still in place today. The cottage next door to the pub in Cross Street was acquired by Wilsons some years ago and was knocked into to enlarge the pub.

By comparing the most recent photograph D taken in 1991 with the photograph B taken in 1961 it can be seen quite clearly that the front of the building has been 'stretched'. The front door is now more to the right and with the building of the extension the fourth window right has changed position and been joined by a fifth window.

*A History of Whitefield Pubs*

*Photograph D: Cross Keys - once a main road pub (photo 1992)*

John Prestley who was landlord in 1871 was fined 20 shillings plus costs for permitting gaming on 23rd October 1871. The case was heard at Bury Courtroom on the 3rd November 1871.

Photograph D above was deliberately taken on the 2nd September 1991, exactly 40 years to the day from photograph A.

Known licensees from 1833 until the last entry in the Magistrates Licensing Records at the time of writing are as follows:

### Known Licensees

| | |
|---|---|
| James Butterworth | 1833 |
| John Prestley | 1871 |
| John Hilton | 8 1 1877 |
| Sarah Hilton | 10 7 1884 |
| Thomas S Hilton | 28 3 1892 |
| Alfred Walton | 22 5 1899 |
| Harry Hulme | 21 7 1913 |
| Mary Ellen Hulme | 7 9 1916 |
| Harry Hulme | 11 3 1920 |
| Edward Mellor | 5 11 1953 |
| Geoffrey M Hunt | 22 10 1963 |
| Fred Reynolds | 4 5 1966 |
| Richard C Price | 11 5 1973 |
| Paul E Cotton | 22 4 1974 |
| Ronald Atkinson | 21 7 1975 |
| Chris E Hopkinson | 17 8 1977 |
| Peter James Reel | 6 2 1981 |
| David Wolfendon | 19 4 1983 |
| Graham Chadwick | 4 6 1985 |

Harry Hulme was one of Whitefield's longest serving landlords with almost 34 years continuous service at the Cross Keys (1920 - 1953) and that does not include his first stint (1913 - 1916) when his wife Mary Ellen took over temporarily (did Harry go off to the first World War?).

*Photograph E: Acid etched window*

Page 45

## A History of Whitefield Pubs

> By all accounts he was a very tolerant man; one of his customers in the mid 1940s who was a youngish chap well noted for his agility used to take bets that he could fall flat on his face on the flagged tap room floor without hurting himself. After he had performed this feat other customers would bet they could do it too and had to be 'spoken to' by Harry who obviously did not want his customers injuring themselves. A word of warning was usually sufficient to stop this nonsense and he never resorted to asking someone to leave the premises.

The Cross Keys has undergone many changes in its structural appearance, but still looks little different externally from almost 160 years ago. Already five times older than the Town's newest pubs, its continued preservation is of great importance.

If we are to retain for future generations documented accounts of the Town's history, then the old inns, taverns and public houses must also be included. It is the Author's intention to ensure that they are.

> The reader may wish to ponder on the fact that Cross Street at the side of the pub was once the site of the Savoy Toffee Works, owned by John Fitton. It was in existence for about 50 years, during which time no doubt, many a worker went to the Cross Keys to slake their thirst.

*One of the first newspaper display advertisements - comedian Sydney Howard congratulating Manchester City in 1934*

## Court in the Act!

From the Bury Times of Saturday June 13th 1857, a report of drunkenness and wife beating in a case heard at the New Bailey Court in Salford:

*On Tuesday last, a stout powerfull fellow, James Allen, of Whitefield, was placed in the dock, and a Policeman stated that on the Prestwich Road on the previous night, he heard a cry of 'murder', and on going to the place, saw the prisoner and his wife. He had been striking her, but was then quiet. When they had gone a little further along the road, the prisoner gave her a kick which sent her into the hedge bottom, upon which he took the prisoner into custody. Not withstanding the brutal treatment she had received, the wife did not appear to give evidence, and the prisoner, who admitted that he was intoxicated at the time, escaped with a fine of five shillings for being drunk.*

## Pants Off - Sent Off!

From the Bury Times, 29th September 1856:

*On Wednesday last, Michael Clough, a Whitefield man was brought before the Magistrates, charged with having about half past eight o'clock on Tuesday morning been found drunk in the street without any clothing upon him except his shirt. It appeared that he stripped off his clothing and offered it for sale to enable him to purchase more drink. He was fined five shillings and costs (sixpence), and in default of payment was committed to the house of correction for fourteen days.*

*Patric Mower was brought before the Magistrate at the same time, also charged with being drunk, and was fined five shillings and costs.* (Author's note: as no mention was made of Patric Power following Michael Clough to the house of correction, it must be assumed that he paid his 5/6)

# Corner Cupboard      Park Lane

The Corner Cupboard, a beerhouse, was at the top end of Park Lane on the left hand side just before the road bends round to the left and the Parkfield Inn.

It became a beerhouse in the 1840s and was in the possession of the Briggs family for most of its life as a hostelry. It was initially thought that its licence was transferred to the Parkfield Inn when it opened in 1864, but it is now known it was still trading as a beerhouse in 1883. A Barret's directory for that year lists Rachel Briggs as a beer seller and grocer. Shortly afterwards a Billy Briggs is known to have kept the place.

The Bury Rate register for 1864 declares James Briggs, occupier and Thomas Briggs as owner and the rateable vale as £15-6s-0d. One story that has survived about the Corner Cupboard is that it was very popular with the local hand loom weavers of the area who also used to play marbles and 'piggy' outside. It had its own brewhouse, but brewed specifically for its own needs.

The actual building which was originally two cottages still stands. It was for a number of years the Park Lane delicatessen and nowadays 'The Village Deli'. Photograph A shows what was the old Corner Cupboard in the mid 1970s (no photograph of the building as a beerhouse has as yet been found). Photograph B shows the rear of the premises. The extract from the 1893 Ordnance Survey map clearly shows the location of the Corner Cupboard.

The rounded-off building at the rear was the brewhouse, now long since demolished. The hedge-privets on photograph B are where it stood. The Corner Cupboard had ceased trading as a beerhouse before 1895, though the exact date or circumstances have not yet been determined. Research continues on this matter.

*Photograph A: Once the Corner Cupboard beerhouse*

*Photograph B: The rear, where the brewhouse stood*

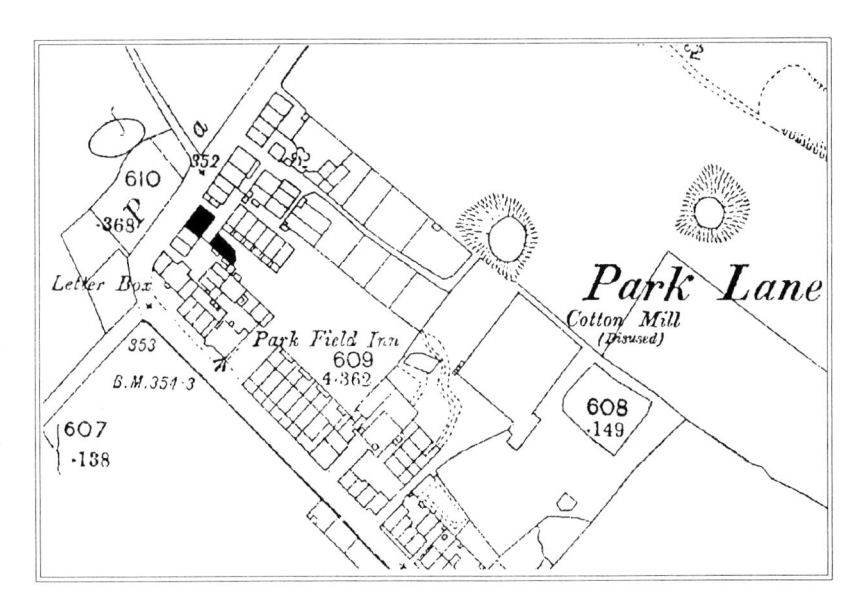

## The Origin of Inns

The word 'Inn' is of Saxon origin and first signified a chamber, although it came to be applied generally to a house or mansion like the French word 'Hotel'. Hence, Clifford's Inn was once the residence of De Clifford Lincoln's Inn, the family residence of the Earls of Lincoln, and Grey's Inn the Town House of Lord Grey etc.

The Inns of Lancashire and Yorkshire before the erection of colleges were merely the lodging houses or halls for the scholars. Similarly, the original purpose of the Inns of Court in London was for the lodging of law students. The real difference between an Hotel and an Inn is therefore very difficult to define. Both are places for the lodging and refreshment of travellers and for hundreds of years hospitality and friendliness have been dispensed by the British Inn, unequalled by any other country in the world.

## Inn Signs become Law

In 1393 Richard II compelled publicans by law to exhibit a sign, though it was not made compulsory for other trades or professions.

The law said: 'Whosoever shall brew ale in the Town with intention of selling it must hang out a sign, otherwise he shall forfeit his ale'.

## The Origin of Arms

There are over 2,000 pubs in Britain bearing the word 'Arms' in their titles. Of these there are around 200 where it is used as if it were merely a synonym of 'Inn'. It originates from the fact that centuries ago the nobility and aristocratic families including royalty quite often owned the inns and taverns or the lands on which they stood. In these situations, the family crest or 'Coat of Arms' of the landlord became the sign by which these establishments were known. Hence, an inn displaying the heraldic arms of the King became known as the 'King's Arms', though the actual names followed much later. Whitefield's very own Derby Hotel, originally the Derby Arms, is built on land owned by the Earl of Derby Estate and to this day proudly displays the arms of the Derby family on its signboard. Bolton's oldest and most famous pub the Man & Scythe displays on its signboard part of the Pilkington Family coat of arms with the family's motto 'Now thus, now thus'.

## Taverns and Ale Houses

Some time during the 8th century some enterprising and reasonably affluent members of many communities opened up their houses to provide food and refreshments, particularly wine. These establishments were referred to as 'Taverns' which is directly derived from the Latin *Teberna*. Although primarily they were 'drinking houses' they were frequented by the upper and middle classes, the poorer not able to afford wine. Lower classes used the odd drinking places which were basically alehouses, the ale being brewed on the premises by the ale-wife. (Ale was brewed from barley, malt and yeast only - hops were not introduced into Britain until the 15th century).

---

174     BURY AND RADCLIFFE DIRECTORY.

## BURY BREWERY CO.,

LIMITED,

### GEORGE STREET, BURY,

Invite the attention of the Public to their superior

## MILD AND BITTER ALES AND STOUT,

All of which are of the highest purity, and supplied in splendid condition.

---

### FOUR - AND - A - HALF

AND

### NINE GALLON CASKS

SPECIALLY PREPARED FOR PRIVATE USE.

☞ ORDERS WILL RECEIVE PROMPT ATTENTION.

☞ PRICES ON APPLICATION.

*Secretary*—WILLIAM MEADOWCROFT.

**Bury Brewery advert taken from a directory of 1888/9**

# The Dragon     Parr Lane

*Built in 1962 its name recalls a local legend*

The name Dragon on its own is an unusual inn sign, usually found as George & Dragon, Red Dragon or Green Dragon. The dragon appears on many coats of arms, notably that of the Tudor kings. However, according to tradition the family of Unsworth occupied the same residence some mile and a half from Bury, ever since the Norman Conquest. The house itself gradually changed from a manor house to a farm with the declining fortunes of the family, but there still remained many relics of the past and amongst them a carved oak table which directly connected with an old legend.

The legend of the dragon of Unsworth tradition has it that in olden times a fierce and terrible dragon ravaged the countryside around Bury, its lair being near Unsworth and which *'Resolutely defied the powers of several brave heroes who would fain have immortalised their name by freeing their country from such a scourge'*.

One Thomas Unsworth, however, a member of the family succeeded where others had failed, by the exercise of ingenuity as well as by courage. Finding that the scaly hide of the dragon made it invulnerable to bullets, he put his dagger into a petronel and rousing the anger of the monster by a pretended attack he shot it under the throat when it raised its head, his dagger piercing the soft skin.

The table was made after this event, being carved as the story goes, with the very dagger which caused the dragon's death.

For many centuries, Unsworth, rich in legend and tradition, was on the far boundary of the Pilkington Manor. Being remote and isolated, the village was essentially self-contained. Its inhabitants went about their business in their own fashion, subject only to the varying fortunes, in peace and war, of the Lords of Pilkington.

Times changed quickly in Unsworth in the early 1960s with the coming of large new housing estates, no longer isolated, with new wider roads appearing, regular bus services and all the amenities of a thriving community.

With this increase in population another public house was needed and in 1962 the Dragon was built. It opened its doors for the first time in January 1963.

Although this new public house is only thirty years old its name is part of the history of the district. By preserving the legend of the dragon this public house is playing its part in preserving the history of the ancient village of Unsworth.

### Licensees

| | |
|---|---|
| John White | 9 1 1963 |
| William Rhodes | 13 11 1968 |
| George A Davies | 18 4 1973 |
| Norma Milton | 13 2 1974 |
| Ray Higson | 8 12 1975 |
| Glynn David Morris | 15 10 1980 |
| John Alan Bradburn | 8 6 1988 |
| Dave Tony Butler | 7 12 1988 |
| Paul Glicklich | 24 10 1990 |
| Paul Thomas Best | 24 7 1991 |
| David James Henderson | 9 9 1992 |

*A History of Whitefield Pubs*

# Derby Hotel

# Bury New Road

The earliest dated deed is one of 23rd May 1860 when the Earl of Derby leased the land to Sarah Sanderson. The lease does not refer to any building on the land. A further deed of 1862 makes mention of the Derby Hotel so the assumption must be made that it was built between 1860 and 1862. This can actually be supported by reports of the Radcliffe New Road being made in old newspaper reports of 1860/1861 which also make mention of the Derby Hotel being built at the same time.

It is also known that there was a previous Derby Arms but it is doubtful that it stood on exactly the same site as the present buildings.

The reason for this is that the Parish water pump is recorded as occupying this site which was also known as the 'marble spot'. This was the meeting place of the local handloom weavers who would play marbles and exchange gossip before going off to weave their cut on the handlooms ('cut' was the proportion they had to complete to collect their wages on Saturday).

**Photograph A: From 'Derby Arms' to 'Derby Hotel'**

The 'marble spot' was also the place where 'Swallow's Circus' was pitched. Here a greased pole would be erected and prizes offered for anyone able to climb it. Singing competitions were also held here. A copper kettle was usually the prize for a winner.

We can only conclude from this that the original Derby was somewhere nearby. Unfortunately there are virtually no records of demolitions for this period surviving.

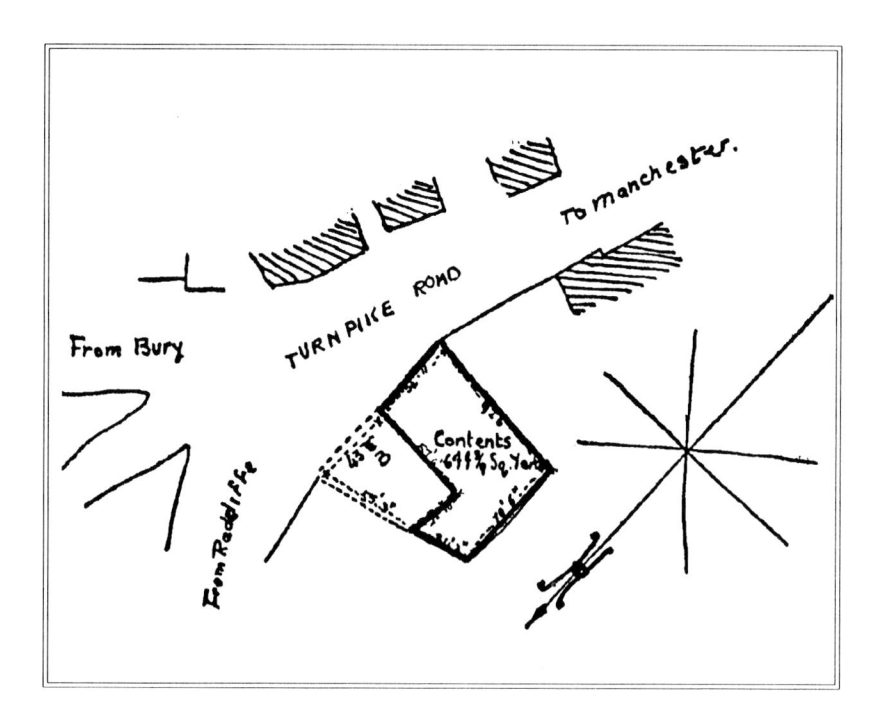

One item that has survived though about this little corner of Whitefield is the story of Daniel Grant. Its relevance is the fact that the Derby Hotel now occupies this place.

> *Daniel Grant (the original of one of Dicken's Cheryble brothers in 'Nicholas Nickleby') was a local businessman who had a warehouse in Bury and another in Manchester. He used to travel daily between the two in his carriage and was much troubled by what he considered to be these thriftless and lazy people wasting their time, which he observed whilst passing the 'marble spot'.*
>
> *One day he stopped his carriage and in an attempt to shame them he offered ten shillings if they would bring the laziest man to him; this they did and Daniel asked him if it was true that he was the laziest man of them all. On being told it was true he offered him the ten shilling note. 'Put it in my pocket for me, its too much like work to hold out my hand' replied the lazy man. Daniel's reaction to this is not known!*

**1877 plan showing the Derby's location**

What is known is that the first Derby Arms came into being in 1838 and is listed in Heap's Bury directory under Pilkington beerhouses. It had probably been a private dwelling or a shop as many beerhouses were at this time and

## A History of Whitefield Pubs

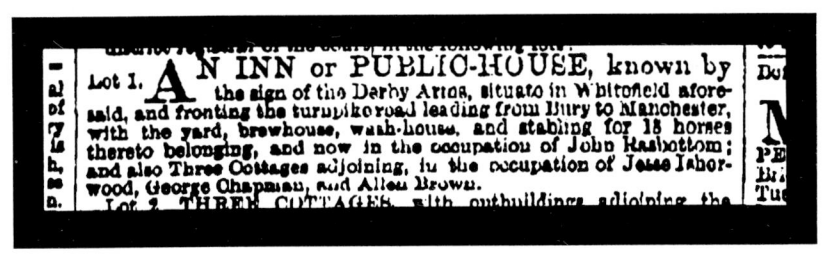

**Manchester Guardian 24th January 1857**

> Lot 1. AN INN or PUBLIC-HOUSE, known by the sign of the Derby Arms, situate in Whitefield aforesaid, and fronting the turnpike road leading from Bury to Manchester, with the yard, brewhouse, wash-house, and stabling for 18 horses thereto belonging, and now in the occupation of John Ramsbottom; and also Three Cottages adjoining, in the occupation of Jesse Inorwood, George Chapman, and Allen Brown.

obtained a licence under the 1830 Beerhouse Act (described in the introduction). The Post office directory of 1843 names Ann Wardle as victualler and shopkeeper, while a Barrett's directory of 1855 names James Handley.

An interesting announcement appeared in the Manchester Guardian on 24th January 1857 (shown above) for a public auction to be held on Wednesday 11th February 1857 at the house of Mr John Mills, The King William the Fourth Inn (see Red King text pp 87/8) at Four Lane Ends, Whitefield at 5 o'clock in the evening. Several property lots were listed. Lot 1 was the Derby Arms.

Although we do not know for certain (it has not yet been substantiated with documented evidence) who the purchaser of Lot 1 was at this public auction, it would be quite reasonable to assume it was George Sorpid, who saw a good business opportunity with the planned Radcliffe New Road and wished to build a new hotel at this important road junction.

George Sorpid held the licence and was also the registered owner of the New Derby from the time it was built until his demise. On 31st January 1875 he forfeited the licence for opening and selling ale on Sunday and the Derby remained closed until he sold out to Sykkes & Company who appointed Robert Reddish as tenant and a new licence was granted on 6th September the same year.

The Chief Constable's report of 1889 records the Derby Hotel as having one spare bed, being able to feed up to forty persons, stabling for four horses and being 65 yards and 314 yards from the two nearest fully licensed public houses. (The old Derby had stabling for 18 horses).

On 30th March 1896 Richard Seed and Company, Brewers of Spring Lane, Radcliffe, acquired ownership.

Dutton's Blackburn Brewery Limited now part of the Whitbread organisation bought 644 square yards of land with the hotel on site on 5th December 1938 (the same day they bought the Albert).

Remembering that Ann Wardle and James Handley were tenants of the original Derby Arms a list of all known licence holders follows:

| Licensees | |
|---|---|
| Ann Wardle | 1838-1843 |
| James Handley | 1850s |
| John Ramsbottom* | 1857 |
| George Sorpid | 1860s-1870s |
| Robert Reddish | 6 9 1875 |
| Elizabeth Haslem† | No dates |
| James W Taylor | 10 1 1876 |
| Richard Hargreaves | 29 9 1881 |
| Richard Griffiths | 27 10 1881 |
| William Vernon | 24 5 1883 |
| William Douglas Burns | 29 8 1889 |
| Robert Yail | 11 12 1890 |
| John Durandeau | 23 5 1892 |
| William R Richards | 22 5 1893 |
| Samuel Nuttall | 30 8 1894 |
| Edwin Mosley | 28 5 1896 |
| John W Taylor | 11 5 1903 |
| Samuel Waterhouse | 5 2 1914 |
| William Walker | 4 12 1916 |
| Walter Wardle | 1 12 1927 |
| George W Morley | 5 12 1929 |
| Albert P Hamer | 8 3 1934 |
| Ellen Hamer | 19 7 1937 |
| Ronald H Hamer | 7 3 1946 |
| John B Nixon | 24 9 1951 |
| Thomas N Berry | 6 9 1956 |
| Kathleen Derbyshire | 26 10 1959 |
| John Boardman | 23 11 1964 |
| Harry Cooper | 18 7 1966 |
| Frederick Yarrow | 3 1 1967 |
| Alexandre Crawford | 3 4 1967 |
| Joseph Farley | 13 4 1970 |
| David S Angus | 7 6 1976 |
| Charles Oliver | 7 2 1979 |
| Tom Tindal | 17 4 1984 |
| Stephen Whittle | 17 12 1985 |
| Michael Buckley | 14 4 1987 |

* Obtained from a local newspaper
† Elizabeth Haslam's name appears in the Licensing Register between 1875 and 1876 but no dates are given; therefore she may not have held a licence

*1893 map showing the Derby Hotel and the Bull's Head. On the opposite side of the road (A) was the Victoria Inn, (B) was the Black Horse Inn*

*A History of Whitefield Pubs*

**When the Derby Hotel had a vault (by Ken Greenhalgh)**

As with most public houses the Derby Hotel has seen of more recent times the removal of internal walls creating the big room effect.

Thankfully the exterior of the Derby Hotel remains unaltered and has fared well in its approximate 130 years. From horse buses to trams and from steam lorries to the internal combustion transport which now thunders past its doors in great numbers. The Derby stands proudly on its foundations, a living part of Whitefield's history-steeped pub heritage. Let's hope it continues to do so for many more years to come.

> John Durandeau, licensee between 1892 and 1893 was charged with permitting drunkenness on the 15th April 1893. He appeared before Magistrates Samuel Knowles, John Brierly and Richard Allen on the 20th April and was fined £5 plus costs.

# Richard Seed & Co.

*Beg to draw the attention of the Public to their Superior* Mild & Bitter Ales & Porter, *all of which are of the highest purity, and supplied in excellent condition.*

### AGENTS FOR
## GUINNESS'S DUBLIN STOUT.

Private Families supplied with excellent Mild and Bitter ALES and PORTER, in Nine Gallon Casks.

**PRICES ON APPLICATION.**

**An original Seed's advertisement for their Mild and Bitter ales and Porter**

**Photograph B: This superbly sign written fanlight above the front door is the original, still showing 'Porter' (photo 1991)**

# Eagle and Child　　　　Higher Lane

**Photograph A: The original Eagle & Child with the present building under construction in 1936**

Nowadays the present Eagle and Child has the distinction of being the last licensed premises in Higher Lane. Its predecessor also had the distinction of being the first.

The original premises was a beerhouse which was part of a row of cottages. It opened its doors to the public in 1802. The landlord in those early days was William Snape (To put things in perspective Higher Lane was only a narrow track in those days and the construction of Bury New Road was not completed until 1827).

It was to be approximately thirty years before a competitor arrived, the first being the original Bay Horse in the early 1830s. Next was the Brown Mare which opened in 1838 (it stood next to Broxups). Then came the Robin Hood in the 1850s, followed by the Travellers Inn in the 1860s (corner of Higher Lane and Bury New Road) and the Foresters in the 1880s.

There were now six hostelries along this side of Higher Lane (by now a proper road). Sadly, five of them have been lost. The Eagle and Child is indeed the last!

The 1893 map extract (below) shows some cottages to the left hand side of the old Eagle. These are still standing, as are the buildings to the right.

Photograph A shows the original Eagle and Child with the present day premises under construction in the background in 1936. The name over the door on the old inn reads 'Ernest Pearson Allen'. His tenancy ran from 1931 to 1946. He was the last licensee in the old pub and the first in the new.

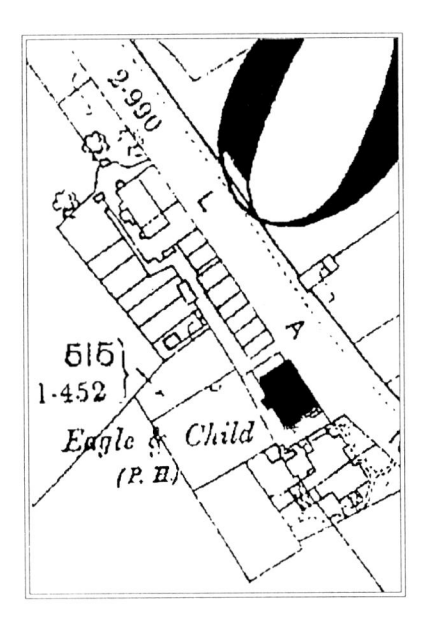

In the 1860s Peter Wardle was registered as licensee and owner. A census return for 1881, addressed the Eagle and Child, Higher Lane, Pilkington, lists Joseph Allen, aged 60, publican, born in Pilkington, Ellen Allen, aged 50, wife, born Pilkington, Rachael Allen, aged 32, daughter, dressmaker, Pilkington, Susan Shaw, aged 23, servant, Pilkington. In an 1883 edition of the Barrett's directory, Joseph Allen is listed as a 'victualler and florist' (it was not uncommon to carry on some other business). By 1885 the new owner was Richard Ashworth. It was about this period that the Whitefield brewery who had for a number of years been supplying beer, acquired ownership.

The Chief Constable's report of 1889 listed the facilities at the Eagle and Child as follows: 2 spare beds, could feed up to sixty persons, stabling for 2 horses and was 275 yards (Junction Hotel) and 195 yards (Bay Horse) from the two nearest fully licensed public houses.

> One local man who used to frequent the old inn was the keeper of the public weighing machine which was opposite on the other side of Higher Lane, up until 1881. He was a well known character and was known by the name of 'Jack Wagg', so called because he was always wagging his head. His real name was John Riley. On one occasion the Headmaster of Park Lane school wished to send a message and asked the scholars if anyone knew where John Riley lived. Only one boy from the entire school answered that he did. If, however, he had asked if anyone new 'Jack Wagg' every scholar in the school would have put up their hands!

The weighing machine on Higher Lane was to check the weights of carts and carriages. If found to be over the prescribed weight regulations, an on the spot fine was imposed. There was another one of these machines halfway between Besses o'th' Barn and Four Lane Ends (junction of Moss lane, Pinfold Lane and Bury New Road)

The inn stayed in the possession of Whitefield Brewery until they were wound up in 1905 (full story in Whitefield brewery text, pp 55-58) when the Eagle and Child became the property of JW Lees (Brewers Ltd) of Middleton Junction. Lees subsequently sold the Eagle and Child to Holt's in 1907.

A section of the contract to purchase reads: *'Lands on the south-westerly side of Higher Lane, containing 3,340 superficial square yards or thereabouts, with a frontage of 25 yards 18 inches, together with the public house known as the Eagle and Child erected thereon. Purchaser Edward Holt, Derby Brewery, Cheetham, Manchester'.*

In 1926 Holt's bought the lease for the land from the Earl of Derby estate.

**Photograph B: The Eagle and Child taken in 1991**

The origin of the name 'Eagle and Child' goes back centuries and has local connections.

### The Lathom Legend

*This popular legend tells how one day, about the year 1355, hearing infant's cries at an eagle's eyrie at Lathom House, near Ormskirk, searchers were amazed to find a thriving but unknown baby boy.*

*The child was adopted by Sir Thomas Lathom, given the name Oskatel and made heir to the Lathom fortune. At the same time an heraldic Eagle and Child became the family crest.*

*Later, Sir Thomas confessed that the affair had been deliberately arranged to conceal that the child was his own son, born out of wedlock, the result of his amorous attraction to a young woman called Mary Oskatel.*

*He left the Lathom estate to his daughter, Lady Isabel. She married Sir John Stanley and the estate passed to the Stanley family - Earls of Derby, who, in acknowledgement assumed the Lathom Crest of the Eagle and Child.*

*Oskatel was not forgotten, however, and received the Manors of Irlam and Urmston as a token of his father's affection. He was knighted by King Edward III and founded the family of Lathom of Astbury, in Cheshire.*

A point of interest here is the fact that the Lathom Crest implied a miraculous preservation, whilst the adopted Earls of Derby crest shows the eagle carrying the child away as its victim. This version is depicted in the windows and on the signboard of the present Eagle and Child.

### Known Licensees

| | |
|---|---|
| William Snape | 1802 |
| Charles Holt | 1825 |
| William Knowles | 1843 |
| Joseph Taylor | 1850s |
| Peter Wardle | 1860 |
| Richard Hilton | 1861 |
| Joseph Wardle | 1 6 1874 |
| Joseph Allen | 1881 |
| William Heap | 27 8 1885 |
| Sherwood J Richards | 12 11 1885 |
| James E Warburton | 11 11 1886 |
| Richard Ainsworth | 27 9 1888 |
| Eli Blackledge | 29 8 1889 |
| Charles Makin | 14 11 1898 |
| James Leach | 7 7 1907 |
| John Butcher | 2 5 1927 |
| Earnest P Allen | 19 10 1931 |
| William Hollingworth | 7 8 1946 |
| John JW King | 10 11 1949 |
| Arthur Simpson | 14 4 1960 |
| Edgar Turner | 13 4 1964 |
| William Worthington | 31 5 1965 |
| Joseph Beck | 30 9 1968 |
| Vera Beck | 1 7 1974 |
| Anthony Smith | 18 2 1978 |
| Andrew Egerton | 26 10 1988 |

**Photograph C: The signboard**

*A History of Whitefield Pubs*

# Whitefield Brewery — Higher Lane

Whitefield Brewery was situated on Higher Lane in the buildings which still stand between Sefton Street and London Street. In more recent times these buildings will be better remembered as the old Woodburn and Spence Garage and currently occupied by Prestwich Motor Bodies.

The arched entrance that fronts Higher Lane (nowadays partially obscured by a huge sign) was once the main entrance to the brewery's cobbled courtyard and stables. The upper floor was the administrative area.

The actual brewhouse is still clearly visible from Sefton Street with its unmistakably original risen louvred roof. This was a specific feature of all Victorian breweries. Part of the original courtyard still exists with access through a large gate on Sefton Street. This gateway is an addition as Sefton Street did not exist when the brewery was built.

The original brewery premises have effectively been cut in half by the building some years ago of a wall straight across the original courtyard. This wall now forms part of the back of the building which fronts Higher Lane, while the Sefton Street half (the old brewhouse) is occupied by Lawrence Brierly & Co, a firm of weavers and braiders.

Whitefield Brewery was founded in 1845 and supplied many of the beerhouses and public houses in the area for the next fifty-odd years. However, in 1898 events started to take place that would involve the brewery in a sensational scandal that hit the headlines in 1905 and ultimately brought about the brewery's closure. The scandal principally involved the Longsight Brewery, the John Willie Lees Brewery of Middleton Junction and the Whitefield Brewery.

*Founded in 1845, it once supplied many local pubs*

*Photograph A: The old brewery photographed in 1991*

The account of the scandal that follows is taken from the Manchester Guardian newspaper reports of 3rd and 4th October 1906 relating to the hearing at the Lancashire Chancery Court in Manchester where John William Lees found himself in the dock.

To understand fully the web of intrigue that unfolds we need to start at the beginning with the Longsight Brewery. This stood on Ducie Street, off Stockport Road, a street which has now been replaced by open ground. The brewery, founded by Thomas Barber in the 1850s, later became Barber & Company and was acquired by Daniel Irvine Flattely in 1868. Barber & Company was retained as the trading name, indicating that the company probably enjoyed a good reputation.

Flattely had spent the early years of his working life in the Inland Revenue Department of the Civil Service before settling in Gorton in about 1865. He managed to combine his commercial interests, which later included a directorship at Bents Brewery in Liverpool, with an active participation in public affairs. During 1885 he contested the parliamentary representation of Gorton against Mr Richard Peacock but was unsuccessful. He also served as a

Page 55

magistrate, being an expert on licensing laws (as might be expected) and was also a county councillor for Longsight prior to its amalgamation with Manchester. DI Flattely died on 22nd October 1897.

The brewery itself had a 25 barrel plant (900 gallons per brew) in the 1890s. It was particularly noted for its porter and supplied many outlets in Manchester, Salford and district. The trustees of Daniel Flattely valued the entire business at £90,000 and set about finding a suitable buyer.

During September 1898, John Willie Lees negotiated with Flattely's trustees, the final terms being £77,500 for the business, £1,658 for book debts and £3,829 for stock in hand, making a total of £82,987. A deposit of £7,750 was then paid. Lees managed the business for a time but ill health resulted in him moving to Blackpool for a rest.

It was whilst he was recuperating in Blackpool that meetings with a representative of Whitefield Breweries began. The whole truth about the subsequent events may never be known, as there were two versions, one originating from Mr Lees and the other from Arnold D Briscoe, manager of the Whitefield Brewery. According to Mr Briscoe, an agreement was reached to form a company by the merger of the Longsight Brewery business with

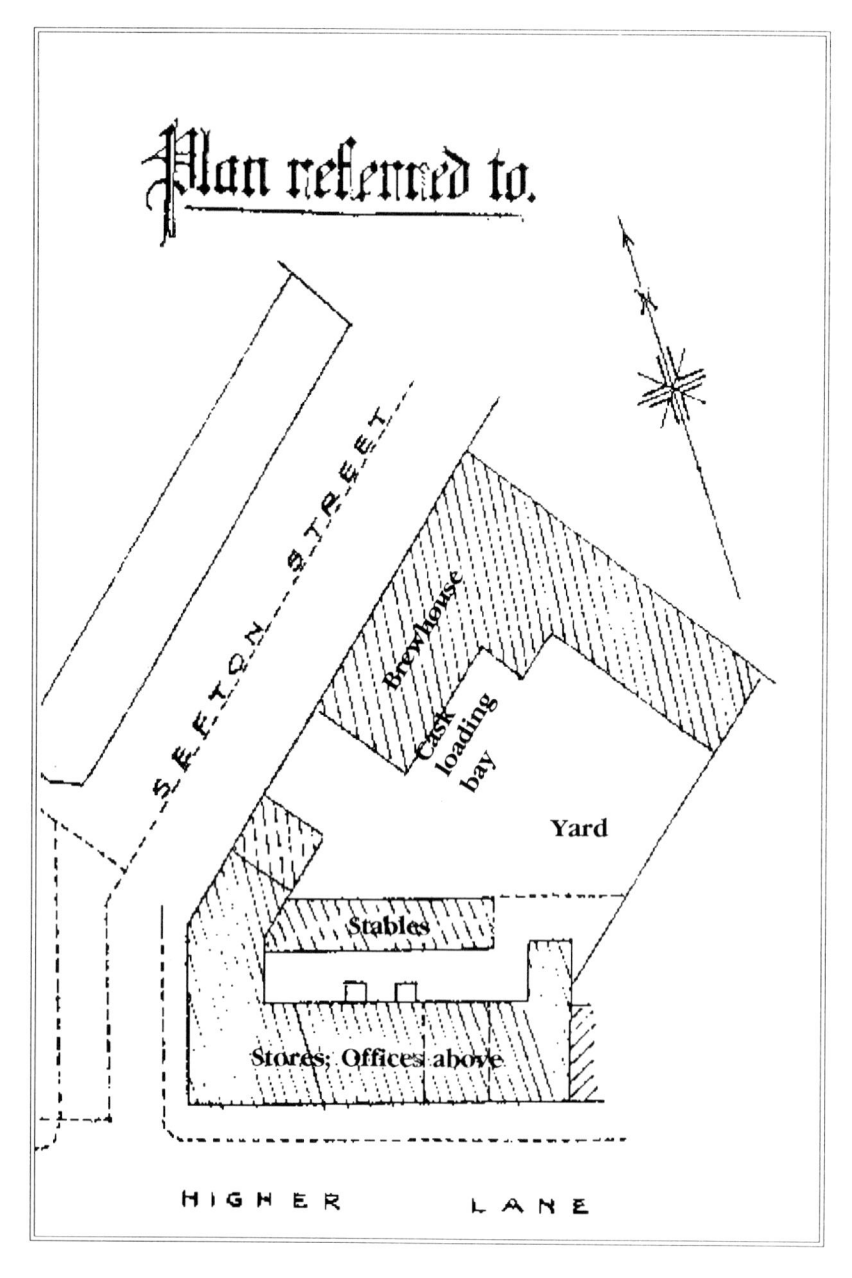

**Photograph B: The Old Brewhouse seen from Sefton Street**

**Plan showing the proposed Sefton Street**

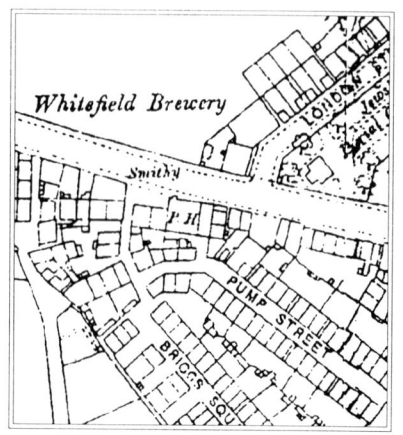

**1893 Ordnance Survey map**

the Stamford Brewery of Ashton under Lyne, Lee Home Brewery of Oldham and the Whitefield Brewery Company Limited of Besses o'th' Barn. However, Lees later maintained that such a merger was never mentioned and that he thought the Whitefield Brewery was interested only in buying the property. What is certain is that Whitefield was heavily in debt. Although they offered £110,487 for the Longsight Brewery, they already owed some £30,000. It was intended that the flotation of the new company would provide the needed capital. Unfortunately for them, the shares were under-subscribed and the new company was formed still in debt.

At some stage, John W Lees was told about the formation of a new company. As he had agreed to accept £40,000 of the original purchase price in shares of the Whitefield Brewery (Lees' story), he then agreed to them being in the new company and also joined the board as Chairman. The firm was registered first as Breweries Ltd, then as Whitefield Breweries Ltd.

In the company prospectus it was claimed that the combined output from the Longsight Brewery and the others would be 450 barrels per week and this figure was used to calculate the expected profit. It was also claimed that the company owned property valued at £153,297, free from all mortgages or other charges. Both claims turned out to be false.

In 1903 a shareholders' committee was formed to examine the company's affairs. This resulted in a winding-up order in March 1905 and a charge of fraud under the Directors' Liability Act. The only way JW Lees could avoid prosecution was to settle with the plaintiffs. He agreed to pay 12s 6d per share and the charges were withdrawn. Throughout the hearing Lees claimed that he had no hand in writing the prospectus and had suffered as much financial loss as anyone else. Despite the settlement, Lees didn't do too badly. The Law Debenture Corporation, who had taken possession of the Whitefield Breweries property when the interest on a £105,000 loan remained unpaid, sold the property valued at £231,000 back to Lees for just £115,00.

The Whitefield Brewery was later taken over by John Brookes. He was the son of a local eminent veterinary surgeon. The family lived at The Hope, a large house which still stands on the corner of Bury New Road (then known as Manchester New Road) and Barn Street. The original stables at the rear of the Hope can still be seen at the back of the Mayfair Cinema (though now used as garages). A census return for 1881 lists John as aged 22, occupation Brewer. In Barret's 1883 Directory he is listed as a brewer of ale and porter at premises in London Street.

In 1962 Thomas Holt wrote that he remembered as a young man, women going to the brewery to buy 'wet barm'. This was surplus yeast skimmed off during the brewing process. It was considered much better for baking bread than the dry barm sold at the local bakers. At the time of writing it has not been determined exactly when John Brooks ceased brewing at the Higher Lane site. Various documents are being examined as part of ongoing research.

The following is an extract from the census return for 1881 for the Brooks family.

James Brookes, aged 60. Veterinary surgeon, Born Irlam o'th Height.

Harriet Brookes, aged 38 (wife). Born Pilkington. (Presumably Harriet was James second wife)

Alfred Brookes, aged 24 (son). Vet. Born Pilkington.

John Brookes, aged 22 (son). Brewer. Born Pilkington.

Fanny Brookes (daughter). Born Pilkington.

William Brookes, aged 20 (son) Vet. Student. Born Pilkington

Reproduced on the following page are actual extracts from the Manchester Guardian of 3rd and 4th October 1906. A few of the words on the original print are smudged.

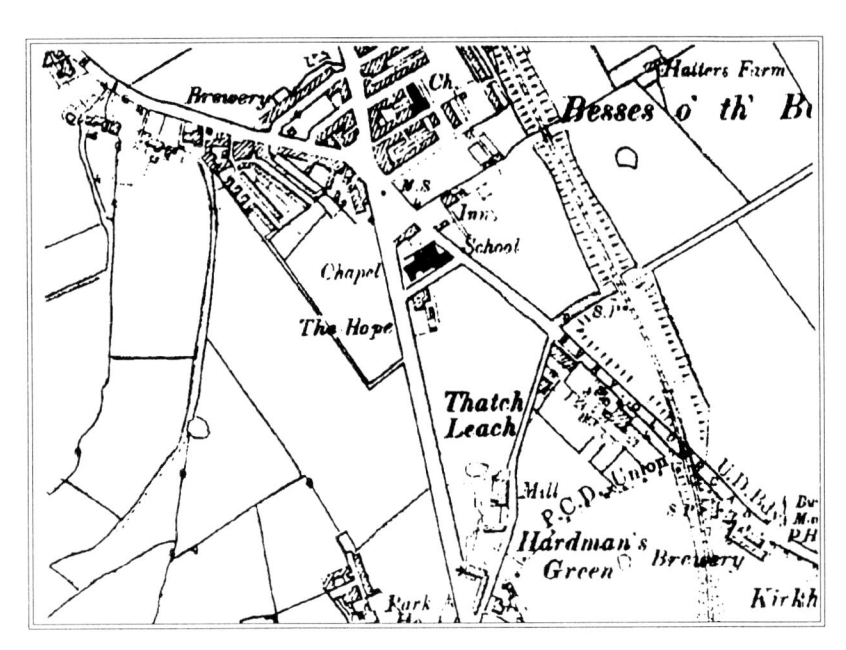

**The Brewery at the top left of this map is the Whitefield Brewery Company's premises on Higher Lane. At the bottom is the Bentley Brewery, used by GF Carrington before they moved to the Clarence Brewery in Hulme The Hope house is in the centre of the 1896 extract shown.**

## WHITEFIELD DIRECTORS EXAMINED.

At the Lancashire Chancery Court at Manchester yesterday, before Mr. A. E. Steinthal, one of the Registrars of the Court, the examination was continued of Mr. John William Lees, a director of the Whitefield Breweries, Limited, by Mr. F. Gittins, the Official Receiver for winding up companies. Mr. Cunliffe appeared for the liquidator, Mr. Grant for Mr. S. Mather, a creditor, Mr. Langdon, K.C., and Mr. Maberly for Mr. Lees, and Dr. C. Atkinson for Mr. A. D. Briscoe, another director.

Mr. Cunliffe continued his examination of Mr. Lees. He said he did not remember an occasion when a dividend had been declared before the accounts were made up. In all cases before any decision was arrived at figures were put before the directors to enable them to arrive at it. The figures were vouched for by the auditors or the

* * * * * * * * * * * * * *

### PRICE OF THE LONGSIGHT BREWERY.

Continuing, the witness said in the March following he was persuaded to take the chairmanship of the Company, under the promise that others would take the positions of managing director and acting chairman. About January, 1899, the Whitefield Brewery approached him. It was not correct to say he approached them, and he said he was prepared to consider an offer for the Longsight Brewery as his health had broken down. They put the value at £100,000. He put it at £110,000, and they split the difference at £105,000. A promise was made that the purchasers would come over in a few days and bring a deposit of £6,000. He knew the Whitefield Brewery had a nominal capital of £50,000, with £22,000 called up. Finally an agreement was prepared for the sale to the Whitefield Brewery Company of the Longsight Brewery and its licensed properties for £105,000, plus book debts and stock, in all £110,467.

That was a genuine sale, not a pure sham?—There was no suggestion of any sham. It was a pure bona-fide sale. I am surprised at the suggestion.

But how were the Whitefield Brewery going to pay £110,000 with £50,000 of nominal capital and only £22,000 paid up?—They said they were going to issue £80,000 extra capital at par, and they were going to get 5s. per share premium. They asked me if I would be willing to accept any portion of that—"leave it on,"—and I said I would leave on £40,000. I said I would have £40,000 in shares in the Whitefield Brewery, and I was prepared to give 5s. per share premium also.

Did you know that at the time they were making that offer of £105,000 to you they were £30,000 in debt?—No.

And did you know they had an overdraft at their bankers?—No, I did not inquire.

Shall I be hitting the mark when I say the object of the Company was to relieve you of the property you had bought and did not want of the Barber Company?—Certainly not; they had no need to relieve me.

You put £30,000 profit in your pocket—I beg your pardon, I never put anything at all in my pocket. I had £30,000 taken out in gold sovereigns.

You got £30,000 profit on your sale?—No, I did nothing of the kind, I only got so much in shares, which you say in your report are worth nothing.

The property you sold to this new Company amounted in all to something like £215,000, and the Company was pledged to find money or shares, making a liability to that extent, in payment. Is not that so?—Yes.

There were two parties to the transaction, yourself and your co-vendors to the new Company and these unfortunate shareholders?—I am one of the unfortunate shareholders; don't forget that.

* * * * * * * * * * * * * *

Mr. Langdon replied that if Mr. Lees was charged with fraud he was entitled to go into the matter. This was a public examination, and his client desired to refute charges that had been made. This gentleman was attacked right and left in that court, and he should have the opportunity of stating publicly his view of the matter.

After argument, the Registrar allowed the questions to be put, and Mr. Lees, in answer to Mr. Langdon, said he paid to Barber's executors for the Longsight Brewery £77,500, plus stock and book debts of value ascertained by valuation, and he received from the Whitefield Brewery £65,000, plus the valuation of the stock and book debts, the difference being £12,500. In addition to that, he applied for £10,000 worth of shares under the prospectus, and had allotted to him £4,922 worth.

Mr. Langdon: So that you had found, so far, £17,522 in cash, which you put into the concern?—Yes.

After that the Company wanted more capital?—Yes.

It owed the bank some £17,000 or £18,000 later on, and could not find the money?—Yes.

That judgment had to be satisfied?—Yes.

And did you buy that judgment from the bank in order to assist the company?—Yes.

Did you find £7,000 for second debentures?—Yes.

You had sunk in this company £29,400, and had a holding of nearly 45,000 shares?—Yes; besides, I also bought shares in the open market.

You held at the date of the winding up 11,055 ordinary and 35,500 preference shares?—Yes.

* * * * * * * * * * * * * *

### FOUR CONCERNS AND A QUARTER OF A MILLION.

In further examination, Mr. Lees said the new Company took over four businesses—the Longsight Company (Barber and Co.), the Whitefield Brewery, the Stamford Brewery, Ashton-under-Lyne, and the Lea Home Brewery. The total sum at which these businesses were purchased was £215,000. He was aware that the total paid-up capital of these concerns was £33,000, and that their liabilities reached £71,000.

Is it not a fact that these breweries were up to their necks in debt, with overdrafts, and properties mortgaged?—They were doing very well, notwithstanding. I do not know they were in debt.

You state that one cause of failure of the Company was insufficient capital at its incorporation?—Yes; that was one of the causes. It was just at the time when people were beginning to look with less favour on breweries. If I had known then what I know now I should not have had anything to do with it, and there are a great many more besides me.

* * * * * * * * * * * * * *

### ANOTHER DIRECTOR IN THE BOX.

Mr. Arnold D. Briscoe, also a director of the Whitefield Breweries, Limited, in answer to the Official Receiver, said he assisted in the flotation of the company. In interviews which he and others had with Mr. Lees at Blackpool Mr. Lees gave them particulars of the Longsight Brewery, and they told him of the proposed amalgamation with the Whitefield, the Stamford, and the Lea Home Breweries. The price agreed upon was £105,000, of which he expected to get £15,000 in premiums on shares. They saw some of the houses but did not employ any valuer or accountant.

The Official Receiver: It amounted to this, that you bought the property on Mr. Lees's word and having regard to the houses you had seen?—Yes.

After questions by Mr. Grant, Mr. Cunliffe, and Mr. Atkinson, the examinations were closed.

*A History of Whitefield Pubs*

# The Elizabethan

## Ribble Drive

Built by Wilsons Brewery and first licensed in 1967, the Elizabethan has not yet had time to acquire a history as such. It became a Wilsons/Watney Mann outlet and then went to Lanchester Taverns and then to Grand Metropolitan who currently lease to the Boddington Pub Co. It's the second time Boddingtons have leased a public house on Ribble Drive. Back in 1882 they leased the General Jackson until 1901 when it became the Albert.

| Licensees | |
|---|---|
| George Hall | 2 10 1967 |
| David Hanson | 18 3 1969 |
| Raymond Shillico | 8 11 1971 |
| David Jones | 16 4 1982 |
| Liam Brown | 15 4 1986 |
| David Thompson | 3 2 1987 |
| Sean Sonnston | 9 9 1992 |

*Photograph May 1992*

# The Frigate

## Thatch Leach Lane

Built by Holts Brewery, the Frigate takes its name from the fact that Peter Kershaw, Managing Director of Holts, served in the Royal Navy and commanded a Frigate.

Excavations close to the site prior to the commencement of the building of the Frigate in 1967 started rumours that an unexploded wartime German bomb was buried nearby. It turned out that the civil engineers involved in the digging were doing exploratory earth work for the M62 motorway which runs to the rear of the pub. Well, that's what they said they were doing!

| Licensees | |
|---|---|
| Charles W Bagley | 5 2 1968 |
| John J Dickenson | 21 7 1969 |
| Robert Rafferty | 2 2 1970 |
| James Wild | 5 10 1970 |
| Bernard Phelan | 4 2 1974 |
| John O'Malley | 2 12 1974 |
| John Egan | 8 2 1975 |
| Christopher Hunt | 28 5 1982 |
| Frederick Allcock | 7 2 1984 |
| John Quinlan | 3 2 1988 |

# Foresters

## Higher Lane

The reference in this name is to the ancient order of Foresters, a large friendly society with lodges called 'Courts'. There were lodges throughout Britain and also parts of America. Like the Royal Antediluvian Order of Buffaloes (Buffs) they usually met at local inns. Whitefield's Foresters has long gone but the name survives locally with the Foresters in Prestwich.

It was situated at number 29 Higher Lane, between the Bay Horse and the Robin Hood. It came into existence in the early 1880s and was a beerhouse only. It had originally been a private dwelling and was owned by James and Mary Briggs who had earlier owned the Corner Cupboard beerhouse at the top of Park Lane. James and Mary lived at Thornhill in Prestwich.

The first licensee was Peter Hilton. A census return for 1881 describes him as aged 48, a beerseller and brewer, so it seems likely he was brewing on the premises. It must have been quite cramped for the census return lists the rest of his family all living at the Foresters as Mary Hilton, aged 46, housekeeper, Thomas (son) aged 18, tripe dealer, (crippled from birth), Mary (daughter), aged 15, cotton winder, John (son) aged 12, scholar and Clara (daughter) aged 7, scholar, all born in Prestwich.

The Foresters was later taken over by the Whitefield Brewery (also on Higher Lane) who supplied the beer until 1886 when it was bought by JW Lees (Brewers) Ltd of Middleton Junction.

It was referred for compensation and the licence expired on the 8th June 1907. The building was demolished shortly afterwards.

*Artist's impression of the Foresters beerhouse*

| Licensees | |
|---|---|
| Peter Hilton | 1881 |
| Thomas Hilton | 13 12 1883 |
| James Howarth | 29 3 1886 |
| Mary A Howarth | 22 5 1893 |
| Joseph Wood | 4 11 1895 |
| Ralph Pearson | 16 12 1897 |
| Robert Ashworth | 16 1 1899 |
| Expiry of Licence | 16 1 1907 |

Unfortunately, after extensive searching and enquiries over many years the author has been unable to locate a photograph of the Foresters.

The photograph shown on the left, taken in 1991 will give the reader at least an idea of where it stood and what now occupies the site. The extract from the 1893 ordnance survey map (page 89) will also assist in this.

*The view today from the corner of London Street towards McDonalds. The bollard at the entrance to Fountain Place is approximately where the Foresters stood*

A History of Whitefield Pubs

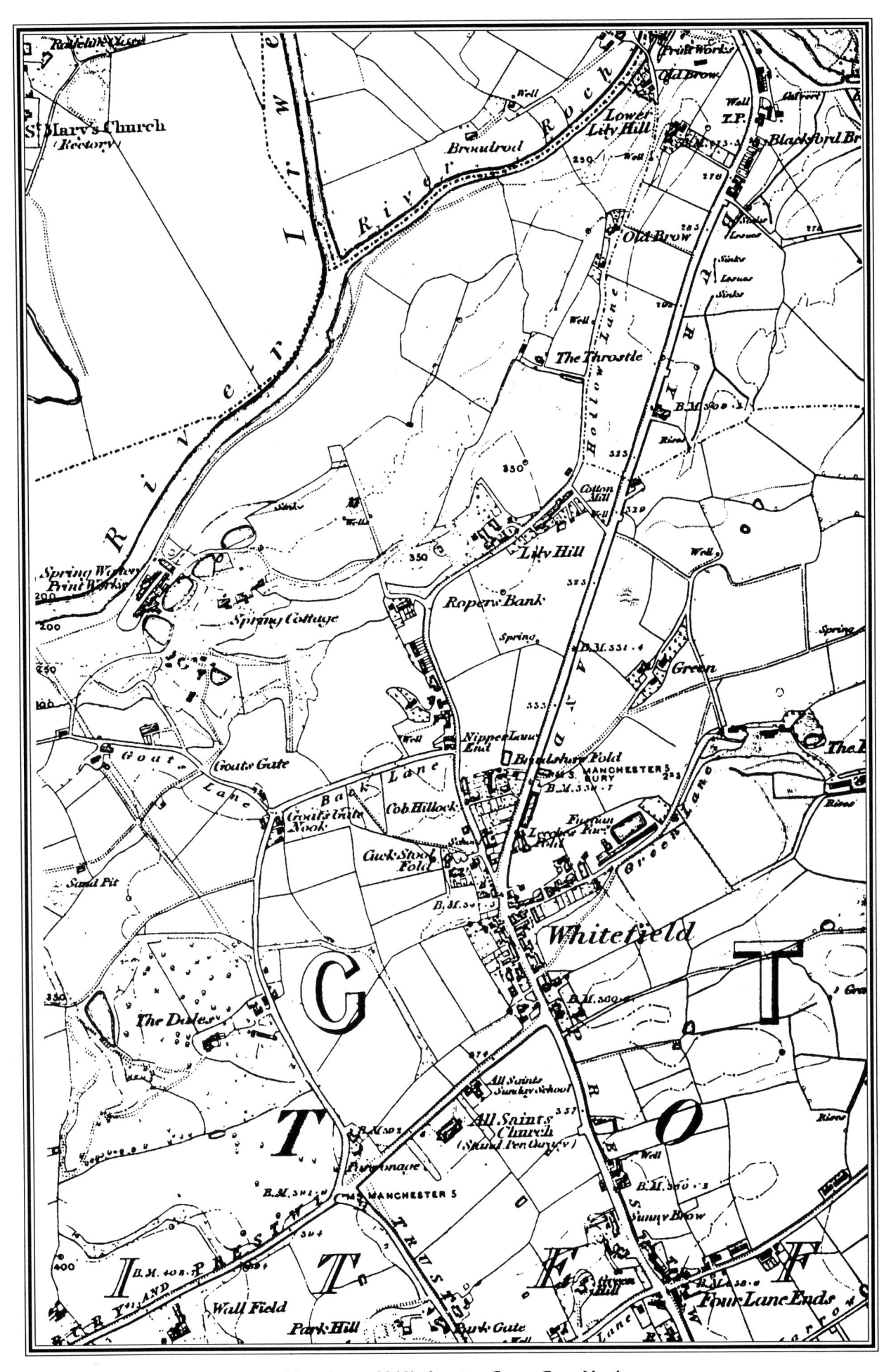

*Map (circa 1848) showing Goats Gate Nook*

*A History of Whitefield Pubs*

# Goats Gate Inn
## Radcliffe New Road

The Goats Gate takes its name from the fact that it is standing on land once known as 'Goats Gate Nook'. This was farmland at the junction of Goats Lane (now Dales Lane) and Back Lane (now part of Radcliffe New Road). Nearby was Goats Gate, a field where goats were kept. The gate to this field was on Goats Lane. The map on the previous page (circa 1848) clearly shows the location.

> *How Goats Gate Nook got its name is one of speculation. A certain Charles R Swift once drew attention to the 'scapegoat' idea, the primitive belief that a goat could take on itself the ills and misfortunes that might affect people and other animals. Swift said that it was country practice in some areas to keep a goat with stock in the belief that this would keep the cattle healthy, all the sickness being borne by the poor goat. He also claimed that another practice was to parade a goat around the house where anyone was ill, so that the disease would be carried away in the goat's body.*

The first Goats Gate Inn had originally been a farmhouse, subject of a 99 year lease from 1816 when it was occupied by Peter Hardman who paid £1-13s-6d per year rent.

*Photograph A: The old Goats Gate in 1962. The side door facing Radcliffe New Road (with steps) was the entrance to the vault.*

In the early 1860s the old farm buildings were pulled down and the new Goats Gate Hotel was built. It was presumably no coincidence it happened to be the same time that the Radcliffe New Road was constructed.

Though it cannot be verified whether he had the new hotel built, the first owner was Walker Hulton, the distinguished Bandmaster during the 1860s of the Besses o'th' Barn band. He was once quoted as being *'a remarkably popular and devoted enthusiast, of a very generous disposition'*. His benevolence towards the band was legendary.

Who the first tenant in the new Goats Gate was is not very clear. The local Justices' records give the name James Dookhorn, but in the Rate Register for 1864 the name is given as James Dootson. This register also describes the rateable value of the premises as £32-19s-9d. It's very probable it was Dootson as this is a still a local name.

*Photograph B: 1962 just before demolition*

*Walker Hulton Esq.*

The Bury Brewery Company was founded in 1861 (the brewery was on George Street on the site now occupied by Quicks Garage). The pubs they built had a very distinctive architectural style. The Robin Hood, Rochdale Road and the Napier on Bolton Street in Bury are typical examples. The brewery also soon started to acquire other licensed premises and around 1870 the Goats Gate became a Bury Brewery Company outlet and remained so until Holts became the new owners in 1914. It is interesting to reflect that Thwaites Blackburn Brewery took over the Bury Brewery in 1949. Had Holts not bought the Goats Gate it is almost certain it would now be a Thwaites Pub.

*In the last world war Holts used cellars at the Goats Gate for storing spirits, having suffered losses due to bombing raids at the brewery and other bonded warehouses.*

**Photograph C: The vault door had two beautiful coloured arched glass panes depicting goats. Taken in 1961**

Shortly after the war on 7th July 1947, Annie Eckersley became the landlady. She had been at the pub with her husband Herbert since March 1930. The picture below is a charcoal drawing of Annie by Ken Greenhalgh. Next to it is another drawing by Ken of a typical vault scene in 1947. Annie Eckersley was succeeded by another landlady in July 1950. She was Hilda Clampet. Hilda stayed until 1956 when in the September of that year another Annie arrived. It was Annie Aldersey and her husband, Jesse. Photograph D shows Jesse behind the lounge bar in 1961 (confirmed by the 1961 calendar next to his shoulder). Photograph E shows the left hand side of the same bar. Two of the original windows from the old inn, similar to the one shown in this photograph (Bar) have been saved and are incorporated into the present building. The Bar-Parlour and Commercial Room windows

**Annie Eckersley by Ken Greenhalgh**

**Vault scene at the Goats Gate by Ken Greenhalgh**

# A History of Whitefield Pubs

**Photograph D: Jesse Aldersey behind the bar in the old pub 1961. Notice the superb 1930s Gaskell & Chambers 'Dalex' beer engines**

are fitted into the wall that separates the lounge area from the Smoke Room. Also visible on this photograph is half of the National cash register till (they seemed to take half the time to operate than the computerised equivalents we have nowadays).

In 1962 the new Goats Gate was being built whilst business continued as usual in the old. Easter of that year saw the opening of the present Goats Gate. On the night Annie and Jesse left the old inn they threw a party for all their regulars. It was free drinks all round. They even had a suckling pig roasted for the occasion.

In the weeks that followed the old inn was demolished. This land now forms part of the new car park. Once established in the new pub Annie started a trend which has continued ever since, namely live entertainment. They had a piano, but no pianist. At the time 'Mabel', a well known pianist was playing at the New Grove Inn two nights per week. Annie wanted a pianist three nights per week. After negotiations with Mabel and William Hesketh the landlord at the Grove, Mabel came to the Goats Gate. For the next five years she was to play from 8pm till 10.30pm non-stop three nights per week.

In October 1967 the Alderseys retired from the licensing trade. Sadly Jesse died recently, but Annie who is now 74 years 'young' still lives locally and has kindly loaned photographs of the old Goats Gate which are reproduced in this text.

How old the original farmhouse was that became the first Goats Gate Inn is not known. Unfortunately no photograph of it as an inn has come to light. We do know, however, the previous building was 100 years old and the present new pub is over 30 years old.

> This sign once hung in the old inn:
> Call at the Goats Gate and taste of the tap
> Drink and be merry but lay off the strap
> (The 'strap' refers to the giving of credit and means 'don't ask for it')

**Photograph E: Left hand side of the bar on photograph above**

# A History of Whitefield Pubs

## Known Licensees

| | |
|---|---|
| James Dookhorn (or Dootson) | 1860s |
| Joseph Burgess | 29 5 1876 |
| Samuel Nuttall | 30 8 1888 |
| Henry Wood | 4 11 1889 |
| Thomas Collier | 3 11 1892 |
| Walker White | 5 11 1896 |
| John Robinson | 9 1 1899 |
| William Mills | 24 5 1900 |
| James Turner | 3 2 1904 |
| Ernest H Ballard | 31 5 1908 |
| Ellen Ballard | 20 5 1909 |
| Charles W Walker | 5 9 1910 |
| Joseph Forsythe | 20 7 1914 |
| Richard Redford | 17 7 1915 |
| Amelia Ainsworth | 17 7 1920 |
| Ernest Webb | 26 7 1926 |
| James H Eckersley | 30 8 1930 |
| Annie Eckersley | 7 7 1947 |
| Hilda Clampett | 3 7 1950 |
| Annie Aldersey | 6 9 1956 |
| Harry Millington | 2 10 1967 |
| George Cope | 4 10 1971 |
| Harry Camilleri | 4 2 1974 |
| Robert Rafferty | 10 12 1982 |
| Patrick O'Conner | 29 10 1985 |
| Stephen E Jones | 9 6 1987 |
| Malcolm Harrison | 12 4 1989 |
| Frederick Anthony Knight | 24 4 1991 |
| John Sadler | 29 4 1892 |
| Michael David Frankle | 9 12 1992 |

After 1850 some cottages were built in the field which had been known as 'Goats Gate'. These were named Goats Gate Cottages. The 1893 map shows these cottages and also the Goats Gate Inn.

Goats Gate Terrace is off Cromwell Road (off Radcliffe New Road) and occupies the site of the old Goats Gate Cottages, although a few are still standing as the picture shows.

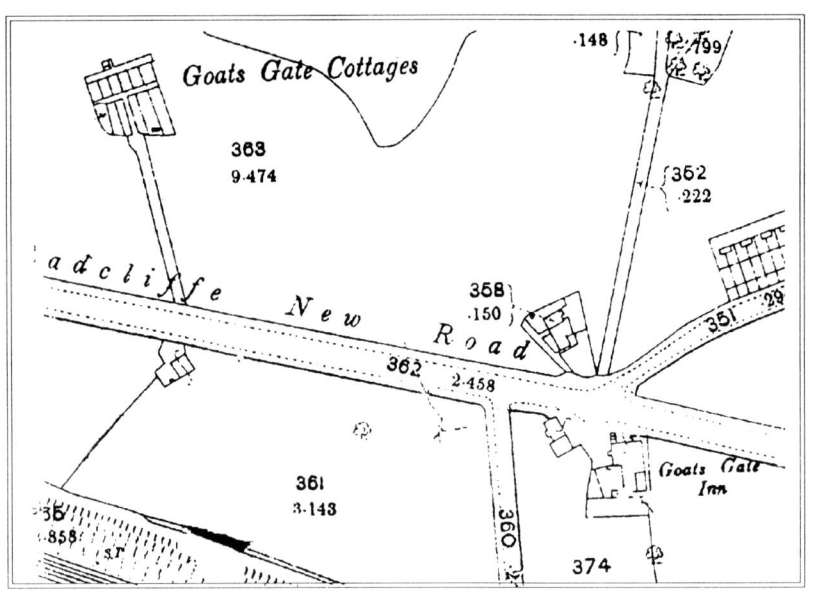

*Extract from 1893 Ordnance Survey map*

*Photograph F: The new Goats Gate just after it opened in 1962. Note the entrance on the right of the photograph marked 'Smoke-Room, Off-Sales'*

*Photograph G: Goats Gate Terrace (photograph 1991)*

*Another Ken Greenhalgh painting of the old vault. Dated 1974, it was taken from some earlier sketches. It depicts a scene which is fast disappearing, due to modern ideas which consider vaults unnecessary.*

*A History of Whitefield Pubs*

*Photograph G: Main Lounge Bar*

*Photograph H: Smoke-room*

*Photograph I: The Vault*

The photographs shown on this page are of the rather sparse looking interior of the present Goats Gate just after it opened in 1962. The top photograph, the Lounge, shows Mabel's piano in the corner, music sheet at the ready.

Harry and Audrey Camilleri were popular tenants of more recent times. The following photograph and text from the 'Advertiser' newspaper 4th November 1982 are reproduced here with the kind permission of the Advertiser. The article was headed 'Spirited Away'.

Hallowe'en will be remembered as a dark night for the landlord and regulars of a Whitefield pub.

For on this traditionally spooky night landlord, Harry Camilleri, and his wife, Audrey, served up the last spirits to their customers.

Harry, 52, and Audrey, 50, have decided to lay the ghost of pub tenancy to rest after a 9-year stint in the town

Now they plan to pump life into a new snooker venture in Stockport.

But even though Harry and Audrey have gambled their life savings into their new hall, they still had to be dragged away from the Goats Gate Hotel in Radcliffe New Road.

"We're very sad to be going," says Harry. "And there's been more than one occasion when we've had second thoughts."

Wife Audrey says that they will never forget the friends they made while living in Whitefield. "We're saying goodbye to many dear friends and that makes it even harder to leave."

At the Hallowe'en farewell night the regulars presented them with a clock as a "thankyou"

# Junction Hotel

## Bury New Road

*A History of Whitefield Pubs*

*Photograph A: The Junction in 1913. Joseph Bleakley was landlord 1902-1916. His name can be seen just below the main roof sign. Notice the open top tram (see Coach & Horses, pages 34-38). The Travellers Inn, corner of Higher Lane is on the extreme left of the photograph). A section of this picture is on the back cover*

The area of Whitefield we nowadays refer to as Besses Junction was not always known by that name. For centuries it was known as 'Stone Pale'. To understand this it is necessary to go back to the conquest of Britain by the Romans around AD 79. After subduing the local opposition to the advance on Mancunium (Manchester) The Roman General, Julius Agricola, turned his attention to building roads, of which Lancashire had four, two running from east to west and two from south to north. One of them came from the present site of Piccadilly towards Ardwick, across Ancoats Lane to Bradford, then over the Heath (now Newton Heath) through Hollinwood and Saddleworth to ancient Cambodinum in the parish of Huddersfield. This road also branched to York.

Another came from the camp at Manchester, running through Stretford, Altrincham, Knutsford, Northwich and Kinderton, from there it continued to Chester and Shropshire. A third road branched off the last, fording the river at Trafford, passing Hope Hall and continued westward to the fort near the river Douglas at Blackrod. The fourth road ran to Ribchester starting near the Collegiate Church through Hunts Bank and Higher Broughton, cutting through the rocks at Stoney Knoll, passing the forts at Kersal Moor and Rainsough. From there to Prestwich, Whitefield, Radcliffe and Affetside, where there is a portion of it left, known as Watling Street.

From there it ran through Darwen and Blackburn to Ribchester. Its approximate route through what is now Whitefield passed close to Besses Junction and followed a line similar to that of Higher Lane.

It continued past the 'Dales' (down what is now Dales Lane) and on towards Radcliffe, fording the river Irwell between 'Sailor Brows' and its confluence with the river Roach. Every so far along these routes the Romans erected stone look-out towers known as 'Peles' or 'Pales'. One of these towers is believed to have commanded the road near what is now Besses Junction and 'Stone Pale' became the name of the district.

The name 'Stone Pale' is actually mentioned in ancient burial records and a Stone Pale Tavern stood on the site of the Junction Inn. It had originally been a farmhouse owned by a John Ingham.

The farm fields extended to an area now occupied by London Street and the land which later became the Jewish Cemetery (now walled in). Other farm buildings nearby dated from 1580. Old documents refer to these buildings as being in the 'District of Stone Pale'. Other references are to 'The Hamlet of Stone Pale'.

When the Stone Pale Tavern first became a hostelry is the subject of on-going research. However, we do know for certain that it was trading as such in the early 1780s.

# A History of Whitefield Pubs

The first mention so far found of a licensee of the inn is of Richard Morris who was the landlord in the 1850s when the premises were listed as beerhouse and brewhouse, cellar and stable with a rateable value of £30-7s-9d.

Photograph B shows the Besses Toll-House, one of the eight along the turnpike road between Manchester and Bury. The reason this is shown is because the Tavern stood directly behind it.

To the left of the picture can be seen the old Co-operative building with its chamfered gable end (see photograph F). This building is still standing and is currently a discount shoe shop.

Notice also the building that appears to be protruding from the right and rear of the Toll-House. It's deceptive but this building is actually to the rear of the Tavern.

This particular building was the Smithy (later a garage) owned by Turner and Greenwood, a firm who ran the Horse Buses between Bury and Manchester from the 1830s until the turn of the century. The garage was only pulled down as recently as the 1960s when the roads in the area were widened.

Turner Street, named after the coach firm, used to run at the back of the inn, but is now a part of the car park.

**Photograph B: The old Toll-House demolished in 1881**

In 1881 with the abolition of the turn-pike trust the old Toll-House was demolished. In the same year the Stone Pale Tavern, now no longer hidden away, changed its name and became the Junction Hotel.

The census return for 1881 lists William Wardle, aged 46, publican, his wife Elizabeth, also 46, housekeeper, Alice, daughter, aged 18, cotton weaver, Mary, daughter, aged 15, scholar and Annie, daughter, also a scholar. All were registered as living at the Stone Pale Tavern in Pilkington.

The following year on the 31st August 1882 it was granted a Full Licence and rose from beerhouse to the status of public house.

Compare photographs A and B and you will notice Turner's old smithy is still there to the right and rear of the Junction Hotel but the buildings further away have now gone. If you also observe the height of the old smithy to the height of the pub, it gives an indication of just how high the old Toll-House was.

By the 1940s the old hotel was becoming structurally unsafe and the front had to be shored up with two huge wooden props to prevent it from collapsing.

In the early 1950s the Crown Brewery Co. decided to rebuild the Junction but did not want to close it down, so as to retain the licence on the site. Miraculously the present

**Photograph C: The nameplate can be seen on the vac shop wall opposite the Junction Hotel. Photograph 1992**

**Photograph D: This photograph, taken circa 1919 was badly damaged and has been re-touched**

building was constructed around the old pub. The official opening of the new Junction (renamed the Junction Inn) was in the summer of 1956, though technically it had never closed!

A metal, downspout rain receiver box bearing the inscription JI (1809) was removed from the old tavern during rebuilding work in the early 1950s. It must be concluded that JI are the initials of John Ingham, the original owner although the significance of 1809 remains a mystery. We have established that the farmhouse had become a Tavern by the 1780s and we know John Ingham had passed on by 1852. Perhaps he simply had the building renovated and gutters and downspouts fitted in 1809; or was it something much more important?

What had once been the old cobbled yard and stables was now part of the Lounge area. Also lost in the rebuild were two magnificent paintings which had been painted on the walls of an upstairs room; one was of the old Newgate Gaol, the other of the Old Bailey.

Strange paintings one might think to adorn the bedroom walls of a public house, but not so strange when we learn that from July 1952 until October 1963 the Junction Hotel had the most famous landlord in Britain. He was Harry Bernard Allen, **the country's official Hangman**! He had (until his promotion) been for 20 years assistant to his predecessor, Albert Pierpoint II, incidentally also a publican. His pub on Oldham Road, Hollinwood, near Oldham, had the unusual name of 'Help the Poor Struggler'. At the time of writing this pub is derelict and awaiting demolition.

Harry Allen and his wife had been tenants at the Rawsons Arms in Farnworth before taking over at the old Junction Hotel and witnessing its transfiguration to the new Junction Inn.

*Photograph E: Harry Allen chats with two of his regulars, Mr A Turner and Mr WH Allcock, as he pulls a pint behind the bar (1963)*

> The collection of old weapons ranging from carbines to African spears which had been displayed in a lounge area known as the 'Gentlemen's room' in the old pub, were put back on display in the new building.
>
> Many changes have occurred since then and it is doubtful if many (if any) remember the collection or what happened to it. Irrespective of this, it was once a much talked about feature of the pub and therefore it is worthy of a mention in this book.

Before he went into the licensing trade, Harry Allen had worked in the drawing office of Mather and Platt Ltd, Bradley Fold. From drawing office to drawing pints, he

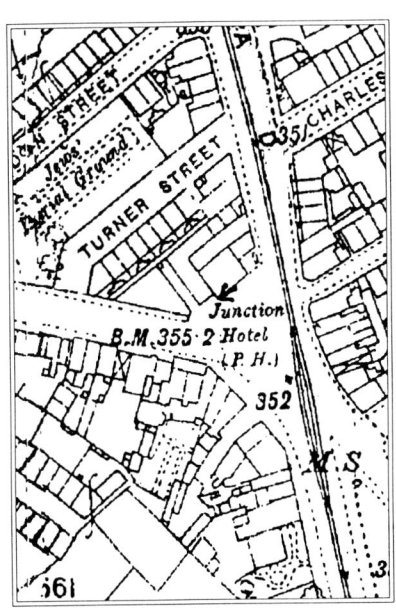

*Old map showing Turner Street now part of the car park at the rear*

*Painting of the new Junction showing the Dutton's signs*

*A History of Whitefield Pubs*

**Photograph F: Just before the 1992 face lift (notice the chamfer)**

became the first landlord in the town to organise trips abroad when he took a party of regulars to Holland in 1960.

Not long afterwards he organised a three day air trip to Barcelona for seventy of his regulars. He even organised free Spanish lessons for them all before setting off. The teacher was his Spanish daughter-in-law, Angeles, wife of his only son Brian.

> Most visitors to the Junction were unaware of the landlord's other profession and this lends irony to many an innocent remark. For example, a passing motorist who had broken down outside the Junction and who had been offered assistance from another motorist to help get him home, walked into the pub and asked Harry Allen if 'he had a rope he could borrow'.
>
> Another tale is of a customer, well known for his odd-jobbing for beer money, being asked by Allen to do some menial task, replying that on that occasion he had sufficient work and could not 'hang around'. Strangely enough, the old Junction was well known to have a trap door in an upstairs ceiling which led to the servants' quarters.

During the rebuilding work at the Junction, some old coins were found in the foundations of the old stable buildings, though the dates were indecipherable. When the foundations for the new pub were laid, Mrs Allen decided to continue the tradition by putting coins of each denomination into them. She is recorded as saying at the time '*I'll probably be wanting that 7s-6d one of these days, so if you see me scratching in that corner, you'll know we are short*'.

In 1963 Harry retired from the Junction. Before he left, a newspaper report at the time stated '*Though Mr Allen is retiring from the business he is to carry on with what he calls his 'sideline' as Britain's Chief Executioner*'. Harry Allen died in August 1992.

The present Junction Inn was the last public house the Crown Brewery Co. of Bury ever (re)built. The age of take-overs and mergers had arrived and the small local independent brewers like Crown became prey for the predators, and it wasn't long before Dutton's Blackburn Brewery Ltd bought 804 square yards of land from the Crown Brewing Co. of Bury on 22nd March 1960.

The deed of purchase refers to land with a beerhouse standing on it which was formally known by the name 'Stone Pale Tavern' but which was now used as inn or public house and known by the name of the Junction Hotel. It also refers to the brewhouse, stable and out-buildings also then on the land.

The earliest dated deed held by the company (now by Whitbread) is a conveyance of 29th September 1852 when the estate of John Ingham, deceased, sold the property to James Bleakley and Thomas Holt. An old directory for Pilkington dated 1818 also lists John Ingham of Stone Pale as a butcher.

In 1975 Whitbread swapped the Junction in a deal with Tetley-Walker who are part of the vast Allied Lyons group owning around 6,700 pubs. To date the Junction has remained a Tetley pub.

When Tetleys took over the pub they commissioned a swinging sign from Oldham Sign Services Ltd of Leeds. Shown below is the original artwork depicting St Peter on the steps to Heaven and Satan beckoning arrivals into his inferno. The sign company wrote '*As this public house*

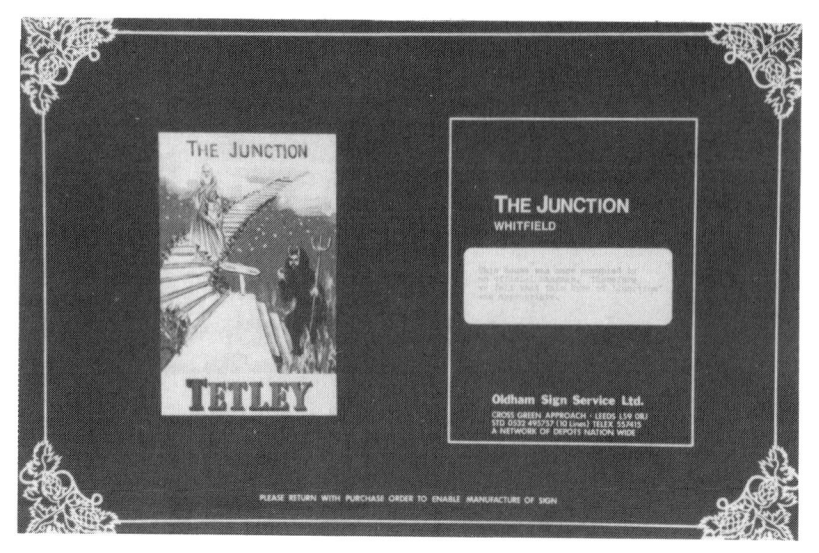

**Photograph G: Original artwork for the swinging sign**

*was once occupied by an official hangman we felt this type of 'junction' was appropriate'.* Tetleys liked the proof design and placed the order and the finished sign was duly 'hung'. Outside the pub, though, I doubt if those who cast a glance upon it ever realised its true significance. In 1992 the Junction underwent an internal refurbishment and external face lift. The swinging sign was removed and replaced with an inapt sign depicting a locomotive. This in turn has recently been replaced with a sign similar to the original.

The photograph shown right, which has only recently come to light was taken outside the Junction Hotel in 1915 when Joseph Bleakley was landlord. He can be seen stood, head just above the windscreen and level with the pub's right side door pillar. The trip was to Llangollen. The charabanc was hired from Lees of Radcliffe. It was shortly afterwards impounded for army service. The old original pub windows seen in the picture were, during Joseph Bleakley's tenancy, replaced with more modern ones (see photograph D). Obscured by the charabanc on this picture are the two small horse water troughs which sat under the windows (later removed). These should not be confused with a much larger water trough which had been hewn out of a solid piece of rock and which had been situated nearby. This larger trough was only removed in the early 1960s when Besses Junction was widened to cater for the ever increasing traffic flow. Coincidentally, it was the earlier increase in traffic that had played a significant part in the deterioration of the original Hotel. Constant shaking of the foundations caused the building to bulge necessitating it to be propped up.

*Photograph H: Charabanc trip to Llangollen 1915*

*To this day, despite numerous refurbishments the Junction still proudly reveals its Crown Brewery origins. Every window still displays the 'Crown' trademark, acid etched in the glass.*

Thomas Holt, a local historian who died in 1962 described the old Besses Toll Bar and the Stone Pale Tavern as the '*hub of the village, with the streets radiating from it like the spokes of a wheel'*. Sadly, nowadays most of the spokes Mr Holt referred to have long since gone. People were dispersed, their houses pulled down, as they were moved to new estates further and further away from the 'hub'.

## Known Licensees

| | |
|---|---|
| Richard Morris | 1850s |
| Edward Nuttall | 1861 |
| William Wardle | 3 9 1878 |
| William Heap | 26 5 1881 |
| Enos Gladstone | 13 11 1884 |
| Joseph Bleakley | 3 11 1902 |
| Jonathan Heap Riley | 9 10 1916 |
| James Clarke* | 8 4 1928 |
| Ian Clarke | 18 12 1944 |
| George Hearndon | 6 2 1947 |
| Harry Bernard Allen | 14 7 1952 |
| James Swift | 22 10 1963 |
| John F Emmett | 21 6 1965 |
| Alfred Wood | 1 10 1973 |
| Frederick Locke | 9 2 1977 |
| Kilburn Wilson | 7 12 1977 |
| Brian J Derman | 12 9 1979 |
| Joseph Dean | 7 6 1989 |
| John William Cotter | 7 2 1990 |

On the 7th July 1936, James Clarke was convicted of supplying liquour during non permitted hours He was fined £4 in each of five cases Magistrates recommended that his licence should not be interfered with.

*Photograph I: Besses Junction before the road widening. The inn is on the extreme left of the picture*

*A History of Whitefield Pubs*

# Royalty and Beer

The earliest British 'pubs' were unpretentious buildings strung along the Roman roads. During the reign of Edgar in the tenth century, there was so much drunkenness that the King closed down scores of Ale Houses and limited each township to one. He also ruled that wooden pegs be inserted in all drinking horns at fixed distances to regulate how much people drank. Any infringement invited severe punishment, hence the expression 'to take someone down a peg or two'.

Royalty have traditionally taken a close interest in the ale houses of England. Pubs built on Royal land were often called the Crown as a sign of respect and the name caught on.

Who said beer drinking was for men only? Queen Elizabeth I used to brew her own potent stuff which left everyone legless except the virgin Queen. According to one courtier it was 'So strong as there was no man able to drink it'.

In past centuries women were sometimes among the greatest supporters of ale. Lady Lucy, a maid of honour in the Court of Henry VIII, consumed a regular 32 pints per day. She drank a gallon at breakfast, a gallon at dinner, another at tea and rounded off the evening with a nightcap of another eight pints.

The Castle in Cowcross Street, London, doubled as a pawnshop. When George IV lost all his money at a cock-fight he wandered in penniless and pledged his watch. Next day he redeemed it and proclaimed that the inn had the right of pawnbrokerage.

Beer was once protected by Royal Charter. Old English ale was brewed with barley, malt and yeast only. So when beer brewed with hops as well as malt and yeast was introduced into England in the 15th century, it met stiff opposition. Hops increased the lift of the beer and improved its character and flavour.

Henry VI, an enthusiast of the new brew, decided to give it Royal protection. He commanded the Sheriffs of the City of London to proclaim that beer made with hops was '*a notable, healthy and temperate drink*' and that anyone molesting brewers would be punished.

Because Charles II and Nell Gwynn could not get a drink at Merrystone, Cornwall, the King commanded that by Royal Charter the Royal Exchange pub should remain open, with plentiful supplies when others were closed. Even today that ruling is respected.

Henry V appointed 'ale conners' - official Government testers to monitor the strength of beer on sale in Taverns. Official posts of this kind were understandably much sought after.

Pub tills were seldom short of small change in the reign of Charles I. The only official currency was silver, so most innkeepers minted their own copper coins. But as farthings were introduced in 1665 and half-pennies in 1671, tokens were finally prohibited in 1674.

Royal Oak is a very popular pub name which has its origins in the famous tale of Charles II who escaped after the battle of Worcester and hid in an oak tree.

## Other Interesting Facts

Courts of law were sometimes held in North West pubs during the last century. Magistrates, according to reports 'were sometimes to be seen inert, supine or asleep as if caring little'. A case of being literally called to the bar.

For centuries pure water was hard to come by and beer was the staple drink at everyone's table. Children in hospital were each allowed two gallons a week in the seventeenth century. Amongst the keenest beer drinkers much have been fourteenth century nuns. In some convents they were given eight pints a day.

An old song goes: 'One hearty guzzle did my body heal, in every gulp I did such pleasure feel, I drank a gallon, slept and so grew well'.

Strong beer with stirring brand names life 'Huff cap' and 'Nipitato' were popular in centuries gone by. An old song went 'He who drinks strong Ale goes to bed mellow/lives as he ought to live and dies a jolly good fellow'.

But watered beer, or small beer as it was known, had its followers too. A man called Ned Ward wrote in praise of it in 1706, saying there was nothing to beat it for curing a hangover. He once asked his doctor to bring him a barrel of good small beer.

Dick Whittington, Lord Mayor of London, was always having confrontations with brewers and paying surprise visits to their premises to try to catch them out. A record of 1420 shows that he even took offence because the swans at the brewers' annual dinner were fatter than his. Miffed, he ordered them to sell beer cheap at a penny a gallon all the next day.

John Brigg a 17th century hermit lived for many years on nothing more than a diet of beer with an occasional loaf of bread given to him by friends and visitors.

*A History of Whitefield Pubs*

# Lord Clive        Mersey Drive

*The Lord Clive was the first new public house built on Hillock*

Clive of India, much a part of British history as Wellington or Wolfe, has given his name to this relatively new public house.

The local connection stems from the fact that Robert Clive (born in 1725, committed suicide 1774) lived for a time in Eccles and attended Stand Grammar School for boys in Whitefield. A house of the school was named after him. He stayed with his uncle who lived at 'Brickhouse' Farm which was the first brick built building in Unsworth.

Built at a cost of £40,000 in only seven months, the Lord Clive public house opened its doors for business on Wednesday evening, 7th December 1967. It also had a large off licence department.

Situated on Mersey Drive it was the first new public house to be built on the Manchester overspill estate at Hillock. It was designed by R Gordon Parry, Manchester Architects for JW Lees & Company (Brewers) of Middleton Junction (founded 1828) and was built by Bleakley & Ingham Ltd, of Radcliffe.

Semi-circular arches and large ceiling fans in the lounge bar were intended to recreate the atmosphere of the British Raj in India during the last century. Authentic Victorian style street lamps in between the arches were bought from a junk shop in Wigan and specially restored for the Lord Clive. The first licensee in the pub was Peter Fairclough and his wife Claire. They had previously managed a JW Lees off-licence in Salford. Another licensee, Mr Brian Dixon who was there during 1975 attempted to establish a Buffalo Lodge at the pub. It was widely reported by the press that it would be the first Buffalo Lodge in the Prestwich and Whitefield area. Now, with the hindsight of research we know that it would not have been the first (see the Coach & Horses text pp 34-38).

The Royal Antediluvian Order of Buffaloes is a worldwide benevolent society which looks after its own members and dependants and contributes to worthwhile charities. Founded in the days of William Shakespeare it preaches philanthropy, goodwill to all brothers, and assistance. Although rarely seen nowadays, Buffalo Lodges could be identified by a Shield outside a pub bearing the RAOB insignia and a pair of buffalo horns. However, after much deliberation between the Bury and Provincial Grand Lodge and the RAOB Grand Lodge of England, it seems the Lord Clive never quite made it. Probably due to an insufficient number of people willing to join the order despite more than 50 members of the Parkside Lodge, in Main Road, Manchester, holding a Saturday night social evening at the pub in March 1975 and explaining to those showing an interest, the functions and aims of the 'Buffs'.

The licence for the Lord Clive Hotel as it was originally christened, was transferred from the Fire Brigade Inn on Pollard Street, Manchester, (off Ancoats Lane). The first application for transfer was made on 4th April 1966, was affirmed on 3rd January 1967. The final declaration is dated 4th December 1967. The Fire Brigade Inn was renamed the Pollard Inn but later closed down and at the time of writing is still boarded up.

| Licensees | |
|---|---|
| Peter Fairclough | 4 12 1967 |
| Gerald Caulfield | 4 2 1971 |
| John Dean | 4 2 1974 |
| Brian Dixon | January 1975 |
| Gordon W Simpson | 9 7 1976 |
| William Edward Oliver | 19 3 1980 |
| David Terence Cassidy | 9.12.92 |

Though the origin of the Lord Clive goes back 268 years to Robert Clive's birth in 1725, the actual building is barely 26 years old. We know modern buildings are not designed and built with the same permanence in mind as those, say built 100 years ago, but let's hope the Lord Clive survives longer than did the great soldier and statesman whose name it bears.

*A History of Whitefield Pubs*

# Masons Arms  Bury New Road

**Photograph A: The Masons Arms circa 1910 Notice the gas lamp over the front door**

The present Masons Arms is the second hostelry on the site; its predecessor, a well known inn during the Coaching era, was in existence well before 1772.

It was known in those days as the **Freemasons Arms**. Just how long prior to that date is not known for certain, as no records can be traced before then. In 1772 William Stock was the landlord and he was there until 1780. It was in this year that the name was changed to simply Masons Arms.

What the exact reason for this change of name was is not recorded, but it may well have been instigated by the stonemasons, who around this time saw their society being infiltrated by non-craftsmen. Whatever the reason for the change from 'Freemasons' to 'Masons', William Stock will eternally have the distinction of being the last tenant of Whitefield's one and only Freemasons Arms.

In the summer of 1815 news of the Duke of Wellington's victory reached the residents of Whitefield and many celebrations took place. John Dawson roasted a bullock in the cobblestone yard of the Masons Arms (bullocks were also roasted at The Eagle and Child, Besses o'th' Barn Inn and the Bull's Head).

It was reported at the time that *'There were ample slices of juicy beef to distribute to the people around and sufficient dripping was left to last a day or two for the poorer families of the district'*.

Like most of the old inns of the period, the Masons Arms had its own brewhouse and the beer was brewed by the landlord. In 1827 the Besses o'th' Barn Band used to practice in a room above this brewhouse and used it until around 1830 after which they moved location a number of times to various places including members' own homes!

Of the many licensees of the Masons Arms, John Dawson was Whitefield's second longest serving landlord with **52 years** to his credit. He was certainly a very versatile man for besides his main occupation of victualling and brewing beer he was also listed in various directories as a wheelwright, blacksmith and dealer in flags (pavement slabs).

Towards the end of 1851 his wife Mary Dawson took over the licence, so it would appear John had passed on. Mary was also listed as the owner at this stage so it is likely John acquired ownership of the premises during his mammoth tenancy.

It would seem that Mary did not stay long on her own because in 1852 a Mary Dobson became the landlady.

On Saturday September 8th 1856 an announcement by Mr George

Page 74

# A History of Whitefield Pubs

Whitehead a Bury solicitor, appeared in the Bury Times. It stated that the Masons Arms Inn was to be sold by Public Auction on Wednesday 12th September 1856 at 6 o'clock in the evening.

*'All that piece of land on the west side of the turnpike road leading from Bury to Manchester, is under a lease from the Earl of Derby for a term of 90 years from 24th June 1814 subject to the payment of the yearly rent of £3-5s.-4d. The premises in this lot are held under lease by Mary Dawson'.*

What happened at this auction is not known, but in 1874 the property was back in the possession of the Earl of Derby.

> At this time, Richard Francis Openshaw was licensee. He was reported for being open for business at 3.40 pm on the 7th March 1875. He appeared before Thomas Wrigley and Jonathan Mellor at Bury Court on 19th April. He was fined £5 plus costs and had his licence endorsed. He was caught again selling beer at 4.55 pm on the 9th May and appeared back in court on the 17th June before Thomas L Openshaw and Edward Micklow. He was again fined £5 plus costs with another endorsement to his licence.

*An old drawing (circa 1901) of the original inn and cobbled yard*

The old original inn was more to the right of the present building, its location now forming part of the car park. This old building had faced Pinfold Lane, Pinfold being a corruption of Penfold. The junction with Bury New Road, Moss Lane and Pinfold Lane was then known as Four Lane Ends and it was here a pen had been erected where stray animals could be penned until claimed by their owners.

On 20th June 1901 Richard Seed and Company of Spring Lane Brewery Radcliffe, leased from the Earl of Derby the land on which the present Masons stands.

It was a condition of the lease that they erect a hotel on the land. Building work was started later that year, the plans having already been prepared and approved as early as 1896.

Exactly what date the New Masons opened is not as yet known; this is included in ongoing research. We do, however, know that Wright Royle was in charge of the old inn whilst building work commenced on the new. We know also that he was the first tenant in the new hotel. We can only assume (giving a year for construction) that it probably opened sometime in 1902.

Wright Royle was there until 1910. This was also the year the Prestwich Nurses Union was founded and the inaugural meeting was held in the Masons Arms on July 10th. This union became known as the National Asylum Workers Union, and eventually became the health care union, COHSE.

The hotel became the property of Dutton's Blackburn Brewery (now part of the Whitbread organisation) who bought 2198 square yards of land from Richard Seed & Co Spring Lane Brewery, Radcliffe,

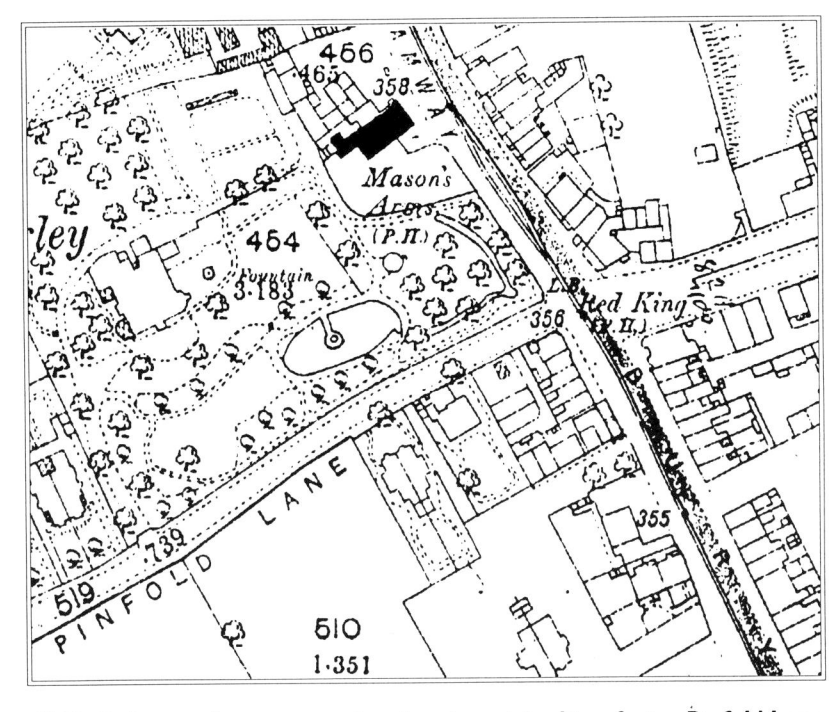

*1893 Ordnance Survey map showing the original inn facing Pinfold Lane*

Page 75

*Architect's plan for the 'new' Masons drawn in 1896*

on 5th December 1938. To date the Masons Arms is still a Whitbread owned public house.

Where possible in this publication I have included extracts from census returns relating to various licensees. Although these do not directly relate to the history of the pub the particular licensees happen to be in at the time, they do give us an insight into the personal side of their lives and their living conditions.

The following relates to John Howarth, the landlord at the Masons Arms from 1879 to 1884. The census return entry during his tenancy describes the occupants of the Masons thus: John Howarth, aged 52, Victualler, Betty Howarth (wife), aged 41, Mary Burke, aged 21, domestic servant, Joseph Hurst, aged 63, labourer. John was born in Clayton-le-Dale, his wife Betty in Radcliffe and Joseph Hurst came from Horwich.

It is very easy to miss items of architectural interest. I suspect the Masons Arms' connection with the Stone Masons and Freemasonry is rarely given a thought, if noticed at all by the people who pass through the doorway, yet this impressive entrance is flanked by two stone pillars (shown in the photographs below) both elegantly carved and decorated with numerous implements of the Mason's craft, a timeless yet generally unobserved reminder of its past.

*Photograph B: Left side pillar*   *Photograph C: Right side pillar*

Page 76

A History of Whitefield Pubs

*Photograph D: Both pillars at the entrance to the Mason's Arms*

In its heyday the Masons had stabling facilities for 30 horses which reflects its importance as a staging post in the old days.

A list of known licensees follows.

## Known Licensees

| | |
|---|---|
| William Stock | 1772 - 1780 |
| Martha Stock | 1780 - 1784 |
| John Hargreaves | 1785 - 1789 |
| Richard Openshaw | 1790 - 1791 |
| Thomas Garnet | 1792 - 1794 |
| Peter Royle | 1795 - 1799 |
| John Dawson | 1799 - 1851 |
| Mary Dawson | 1851 |
| Mary Dobson | 1852 |
| John Davison | 1864 |
| Richard Horrocks | (no dates) |
| Richard Openshaw | 24 2 1874 |
| William Place | 4 9 1876 |
| John Howarth | 16 1 1879 |
| Benjamin Webster | 10 7 1884 |
| James Webster | 1895 |
| Arbaham Smethurst | 20 5 1901 |
| Wright Royle | late 1901 |
| Septimus Walkden | 29 12 1910 |
| Thomas Topping | 16 12 1915 |
| Lillian Topping | 7 9 1916 |
| Thomas Topping | 13 2 1919 |
| John Green | 1 5 1919 |
| Wallace Atkinson | 3 5 1926 |
| Joseph G Heys | 23 7 1934 |
| Edward Taylor | 24 4 1941 |
| David D Parkinson | 6 11 1944 |
| Eliza Dyson | 9 7 1945 |
| Eric Pilkington | 3 4 1950 |
| Percy Harrison | 3 6 1954 |
| Walter Brooks | 3 2 1955 |
| Eric Walker | 3 9 1963 |
| Ernest FL Vaughan | 10 11 1969 |
| David J Brown | 22 4 1974 |
| Victor J Ellis | 19 7 1976 |
| James H Wilson | 13 9 1978 |
| Anthony Rice | 6 2 1980 |
| Ray Bowen | 29 10 1982 |
| Philip C Spears | 14 4 1987 |
| David Taylor | 13 4 1988 |
| Philip Adrian Camilleri | 13 9 1989 |
| Kevin Carl Csonge | 11 3 1992 |
| Robert Anthony O'Neill | 9 12 1992 |

*Manchester Evening News article Friday 26th November 1982*

**DON'T put on your jeans if you want a pint at the Masons Arms — the landlord is banning all denim-clad customers.**

His move, which has baffled jeans manufacturers, has been backed by brewers Whitbread who are spending £30,000 sprucing up the Whitefield pub.

Ray Bowen, the new landlord at the 100-year-old hostelery, built on the site of an ancient staging post, has made his stand against the 20th century fashion after trouble with young customers.

He said: "It got to the stage where most of the regulars were skinheads or bikers or were just scruffily dressed in jeans and pumps. Although it might offend some people, I had to do something."

Notices outside the Bury New Road pub state that when it reopens next month after its facelift only smartly dressed customers will be served. The notices point out that jeans, trainers and leathers will be banned.

Mr Bowen, aged 37, said: "I have had trouble here almost every night with fights and aggravation I can do without. It's like a meeting place for unruly elements. Older, nicer customers look in and then move on somewhere else.

"We want sensible people, married couples and others not looking for trouble. It's not too much of a problem to slip on a pair of slacks when you go out rather than denims."

Mr Bowen has been at the pub two months. He estimates that in that time 90 per cent of his customers have been young people.

### Horrified

Bosses at a major jeans company are horrified at the ban which they believe is the first imposed by a British pub. However, many clubs ban denims.

Mr Miles Templeman, marketing director for Levi Strauss, said: "The landlord's decision is very puzzling. He is sure to lose a lot of custom. Forty million pairs of jeans are sold in this country each year — half of them to people aged 15-24 who buy two or three pairs annually."

One person who does wear denims is Mr Bowen's boss — the brewery's area manager, Mr Ian Webster. He said: "I fully support the landlord who is making a strong point about standards of dress. I normally wear my jeans in the garden and I certainly won't be wearing them when I visit the Masons."

During its facelift, the pub is shut in the evening but opens at lunchtime for business in an upstairs room

*Mr & Mrs Bowen (1982)*

## Of More Recent Times

Controversy surrounded the Masons eleven years ago when the licensee, Mr Ray Bowen decided to ban people who wore jeans. The newspaper clipping, right, is taken from the Manchester Evening News, Friday 26th November 1982. The article appeared under the headline 'Jeans veto to end pub aggro'. Coincidentally, Mr Miles Templeman (mentioned in the article) went on to become the Managing Director of Whitbread!

*The Masons Bar, K. Greenhalgh (1972)*

Page 77

# New Grove Inn — Bury New Road

*Photograph A: The Grove in the 1950s (notice the cottages right)*

The Concise English dictionary defines Grove as a small wood or group of trees; years ago there were many such small wooded areas in the Parish of Pilkington, as indeed there were elsewhere. The original old inn was built in just such a picturesque setting and from becoming the inn in the grove became known simply as the Grove Inn. It was quite common in those days to base the names of local hostelries on their geographical location or surroundings. Local examples of this practice are the Junction Hotel at Besses Junction. The Bridge Inn, next to Blackford Bridge. The Church Inns at Whitefield and Prestwich, Parkside Hotel opposite Heaton Park and the Goats Gate Inn (see text pp 62-66).

The present new Grove was built in the early 1920s and replaced the original Grove Inn which stood further back from the road than the present building.

Photograph A (above) shows the old cottages facing Pinfold Lane that used to stand at the side of the pub. The original Cooksons Cycle Shop was in one of these old properties. Notice also the no 'Holts Ales' signs anywhere on the building. This was typical of many Holts pubs years ago.

At the side of the old building was a stable where the Whitefield Mail-Gig was kept. This used to collect the mail twice daily from the pillar box which stood in front of the old Toll-House at Besses. In those days the Post Office was on the corner of Heap Street (opposite the Junction Hotel) and was kept

*Photograph B: William Hesketh, landlord 1959 - 1970*

# A History of Whitefield Pubs

**Photograph C: One of the superb acid etched windows**

by Mr WF Hunter. He was followed by Mr F Eckersall who set up a new Post Office on Higher Lane, next door but one to the Travellers Inn. His father, Alfred Eckersall, had the clog shop which adjoined the inn (see Travellers text on pages 92/3)

In the early 1860s Samuel Williamson was the tenant though Richard Jones is listed as the owner and in 1874 he took over the running of the place himself. He was also a tenor-horn player in Besses o'th' Barn Band and used to permit the band to practice in the old store room which was attached to the building. An old story that has survived about one of these practice sessions is of the bandsman who was late for the practice and was walking up Bury New Road towards the Grove. As he got near he could hear the band playing and thought to himself how good it sounded. On entering the practice room he waited for the band to rest their instruments and then told them how he had heard them from a distance and how good it sounded. Back came the reply *'If that's the case maybe we should all stand outside and have a listen'*!

The rate register for 1864 lists the Grove as 'beerhouse, cellar, kitchen and stable. Rateable value £15-6s-0d'. Edward Holt purchased the Grove in 1907. Part of the contract to purchase reads:

*'Land on the westerly side of Bury New Road, Whitefield, containing 924 superficial square yards or thereabouts, with a frontage of 25 yards 9 inches, together with the buildings known as the 'Grove Inn' erected thereon.'*

In 1925 Holts Brewery bought the land from the Earl of Derby Estate on which the pub stands.

From the list of licensees it can be seen that the Grove has had four very long serving tenants with over 90 years service between them, and they were

- William Jones     28 years
- Thomas Livesey   19 years
- Harry Higson     22 years
- Leslie Mitchell    22 years

A list of the known tenants including the four mentioned follows below

## Known Licensees

| | |
|---|---|
| Samuel Williamson | early 1860s |
| Richard Jones | 31 8 1874 |
| William Jones | 9 11 1876 |
| Thomas Livesey | 18 4 1904 |
| Mary Alice Beswick | 7 5 1923 |
| John A Higson | 3 9 1931 |
| Emily Higson | 19 7 1937 |
| Harry Higson | 26 8 1937 |
| William Hesketh | 10 9 1959 |
| Leslie Mitchell | 20 7 1970 |
| Ian Hart | 22.7.1992 |

Photograph D below shows the pub nowadays, nestling in foliage, reminiscent of its forerunner, the inn in the grove.

**Photograph D: The Grove nowadays (photo 1991)**

Page 79

*A History of Whitefield Pubs*

# Parkfield Inn
## Park Lane

On 24th January 1857 an announcement appeared in the Manchester Guardian for an auction to be held at the King William the Fourth Inn at Four Lane Ends (see also Red King text) on Wednesday 11th February 1857. Lot 3 was a plot of land on the easterly side of Park Lane in Whitefield, formerly a parcel of land known by the name of '**Parkfield**' and also three cottages erected thereon. There were also other properties included in this lot (see original newspaper clipping below).

The first mention of The Parkfield as an inn comes in 1864 where it is listed in the Rate book for that year as the Parkfield Inn, Park Lane, with a kitchen, stable and cellar, rateable value £45-13s-9d. Whether or not the original inn was made up from the 'three cottages erected thereon' is not very clear. The available surviving documentation is very limited with regard to such details. It is commonly thought that the existing building was probably erected just prior to 1864.

The first owner was William Knott and Samuel (his son?) appears to be the first licensee, starting at 1864. Margaret Knott took over the licence in 1880 and also become the registered owner, which implies that William and Samuel had passed on and Margaret had inherited the inn.

She is also listed in the Barret's Directory for 1883 as a victualler so perhaps she was brewing there as well. By 1885 Margaret's daughter Elisa Anne Knott is the holder of the licence. The Chief Constable's report of 1889 listed the Parkfield as having no spare beds for travellers, facilities to feed up to 30 persons and stabling for four horses. In the late 1890s Margaret Knott sold the Parkfield Inn to Richard Seed and Company, Spring Lane Brewery, Radcliffe (founded in 1827).

*Photographed here in 1982*

The property was then bought by Dutton's as part of a multiple transaction from Seed's on 5th December 1938. The purchase included the adjacent cottage, number 74 Park Street. Dutton's were then taken over by Whitbread in 1964 who still own the pub.

In 1968 a plot of land to the left of the inn was purchased by the brewery and is now used as a car park.

### Known Licensees

| | |
|---|---|
| Samuel Knott | 1864 |
| Margaret Knott | 27 5 1880 |
| Elisa Anne Knott | 27 1 1885 |
| John R Potter | 27 3 1890 |
| Willis Howarth | 28 8 1890 |
| Richard Hall | 20 5 1901 |
| Nathan Horrocks | 19 12 1903 |
| Mary Anne Horrocks | 8 9 1910 |
| Abraham Smethurst | 29 12 1910 |
| William Walker | 7 5 1914 |
| Alfred Walton | 14 12 1916 |
| Clara Walton | 14 3 1918 |
| William Williams | 8 1 1923 |
| Thomas Farrimond | 2 6 1927 |
| Ernest Taylor | 6 1 1930 |
| George Adams | 16 11 1944 |
| James Austin | 7 7 1947 |
| Lily Dickenson | 2 2 1950 |
| John Hall | 28 7 1958 |
| Ralph G Doughty | 19 7 1962 |
| James Stanworth | 22 10 1963 |
| William D Beswick | 6 10 1969 |
| Tom G Tindall | 1 10 1973 |
| Joseph Tomlinson | 8 6 1977 |
| Peter Wilkinson | 29 10 1982 |
| Trevor D Lewis | 18 4 1990 |

*Extract from the Manchester Guardian 24th January 1857*

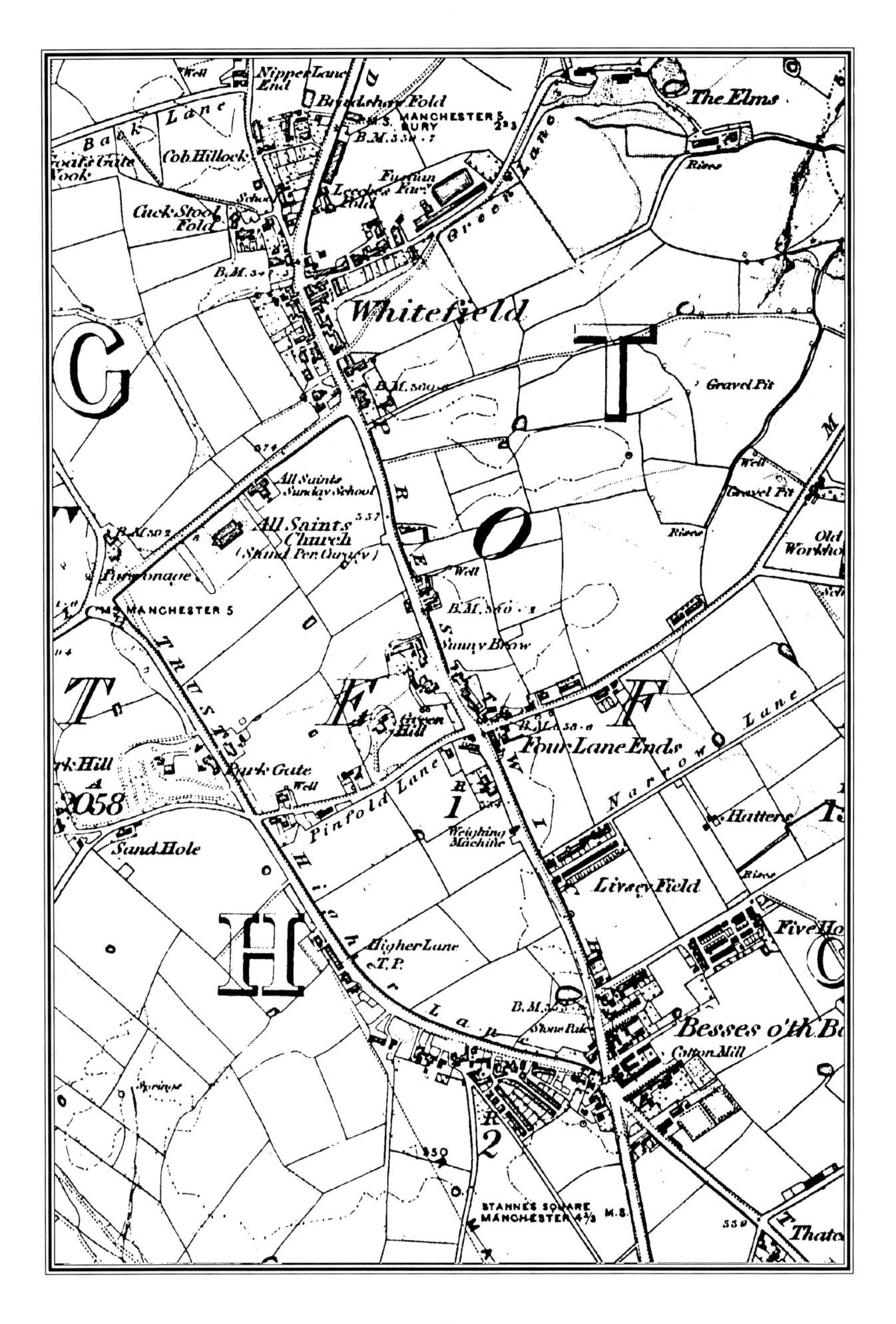

*1848 map of Whitefield showing more of the southern end of the town than that shown on page 61*

*A History of Whitefield Pubs*

# Queen Anne  Hollins Lane, (late Chapel Lane)

*Photograph A: Photographed here sometime in the 1940s*

Queen Anne was born in 1665, daughter of James II. She succeeded William, husband of her sister Mary and became Queen in 1702. She had seventeen children and died in 1714 without surviving issue, last of the Stuart line. Nevertheless, Unsworth's Queen Anne is still going strong and can be seen in the photograph above sporting her Bury Brewery Company Livery in the 1940s.

Alfred Clogg was the first owner and a Pilkington directory for 1818 tells us that Wright Duckworth was the licensee that year. As he is also listed as a victualler, he was probably brewing on the site. Clogg sold the property to the Earl of Derby Estate around 1880. They in turn leased it to the Bury Brewery Company (founded in 1861). In 1925 the brewery purchased the property outright. In 1949 Thwaites Brewery of Blackburn took over the Bury Brewery Company who at that time had 80 licensed houses.

The Queen Anne remains to this day a Thwaites House. Daniel Thwaites was founded in 1807 as Duckworth & Clayton and registered in March 1897 as Daniel Thwaites. It is still an independent brewery with around 415 tied houses in (mainly) Lancashire and Cheshire.

Regrettably both the deeds and Thwaites' own files throw very little light into the structural history of the Queen Anne, so let's observe our own.

To the untrained eye, after looking at the photograph taken in the 1940s and the present day

*Photograph B: The Queen Anne in 1962*

*A History of Whitefield Pubs*

***Photograph C: The Queen Anne (October 1992) shows the many changes which have taken place***

photograph, the assumption could be made that it must have been rebuilt. However, by comparing the three photographs carefully it will be realised that it was not, though some dramatic changes have taken place, not only to the pub, but to the surrounding area also.

The most obvious change is the roof line, the stone and brickwork fascia bearing the name 'Queen Anne' has been removed along with the tall chimneys, which must have been done after 1962. The photograph for that year, though not very clear, shows little change since the 1940s, except that the 'Bury Brewery House' sign on the gable end has been repainted to read 'Thwaites Ales' and additional Thwaites signs fixed above the front door. Comparing the early photograph with the latest we can see that the window frames don't appear to have altered and though not actually visible on the photo above, the original ornate acid etched 'Queen Anne' windows are still in place. The stone door surround is the most obvious clue that behind the changed exterior, the old Queen Anne is still with us.

Other obvious differences between the earlier photograph and the latest are the addition to a single storey extension on the left gable, the trees (and lamp post) on the right hand side, the swinging sign above the front door and the pebble dashing of the lower half.

One more piece of information to add to this potted history of the Queen Anne is the entry in the Chief Constable's report of 1889 relating to the facilities offered by the region's fully licensed public houses. The Queen Anne is recorded as having stabling facilities for two horses and one spare bed for any weary traveller who decided to stay overnight. Amazingly, the report said that this particular hostelry could feed up to 100 persons at one sitting.

We know the inn was trading as such in 1818 and a list of all the known licensees from that year follows. The names prior to 1869 are taken from a variety of directories (local licensing records didn't start until then). There may have been other licensees as well as the ones listed. Unfortunately, however, directories for certain years have not survived. As with all other lists of licensees in this book the Author does not claim it to be comprehensive.

### Known Licensees

| | |
|---|---|
| Wright Duckworth | 1818 |
| James Crook | 1843 |
| Simon Partington | 1850 |
| James Hamilton | 1858 - 1861 |
| Thomas Jackson | 1861 |
| Sarah Jackson | 18 7 1884 |
| Margaret Berry | 20 5 1901 |
| Stanley Berry | 8 2 1912 |
| MA Mather | 4 9 1916 |
| Stanley Berry | 13 3 1919 |
| Thomas Levitt | 4 3 1932 |
| Margaret Ann Levitt | 26 7 1933 |
| Ernest Neely | 21 6 1950 |
| John Patefield | 10 8 1955 |
| James Hamer | 26 9 1956 |
| Samuel Lee | 7 1 1959 |
| Samuel Sewell | 14 10 1970 |
| Lawrence McGinty | 19 7 1976 |
| William Bryceland | 7 12 1988 |
| Michael Barry Clempner | 8 9 1993 |

A music licence was granted on the 19th June 1957 for piano and drums in the lounge

*A History of Whitefield Pubs*

# Robin Hood  Higher Lane

**Photograph A: Sometime between February 1907 - September 1915. The bay window was added after 1893**

The Robin Hood on Higher Lane stood opposite what is nowadays a discount shoe store in the old Co-operative buildings which stand next to the Junction Inn. Because of its proximity to the Besses road junction it was always one of the town's more popular alehouses.

Originally two cottages, it opened in the 1850s, the registered owner at the time being Nathan Crompton. He was a well known local businessman who was also listed in local directories as a building contractor. In 1874 he appointed Ellis Hill as tenant. Ellis had previously run a beerhouse known as the Spotted Cow.

## The Spotted Cow

Unfortunately the old licensing register and Rate register likewise only gives its address as Whitefield and research has not as yet discovered exactly where the Spotted Cow was.

We do, however, know from the licensing register that on the 6th of September 1869 the offence of permitting drunkenness was committed at the establishment. On 14th October 1869 the owner, a Mr George Richardson who only gave his address as Lilyhill, appeared before Captain Mellor, the Magistrate at Bury and was fined five shillings (25p). No more entries beyond 1869 appear in the Licensing register and two black lines running diagonally across the page have the words 'Pulled Down' written between them. We must conclude that was the end of the Spotted Cow as the name never appears again.

What Ellis Hill did between 1869 and 1874 when he took charge of the Robin Hood we shall never know, but from this point on the Hill family were to be connected with the Robin Hood for the next 30 years. Boddington's Brewery acquired the place in the 1870s but who supplied the beer before then is not known. Perhaps it was Whitefield Brewery; it was practically on the doorstep!

All pubs have their characters whether it be the landlord, a member of the staff or a customer. The Robin Hood was no exception. In 1921 Robert Farrand was the tenant. Apart from being an alehouse keeper he was also a professional French polisher. He had a contract with a local undertaker and was obliged to polish so many coffins a week, a difficult task one might think. How do you run a busy beerhouse and polish coffins as well? Robert solved the problem by having the unpolished items delivered to the pub. He then laid them across the tables in the Tap Room and merrily French polished away, able to serve and keep his eye on his customers at the same time. The undertakers that supplied Bob Farrand with unpolished coffins is thought to be Jacksons who were situated at the bottom of Livesey Street. They made their own coffins and the timber was a common sight left out in the yard to season.

Mrs Louie Schofield is the daughter of Clarence and Bertha Briggs who took over at the Robin Hood when Robert Ferrand retired. She was nine years old then. Now at 78 she recalls

'Bob Farrand frightened a lot of the customers away. Fancy going for a drink and having to look at a room full of coffins'.

Louie lived at the pub and has many fond memories of the place. She has some sad ones too. It was in 1935 that Boddingtons were given a choice to close down one of their pubs in the area under the 1904 Compensation Act (see introduction). It was to be either the Red King or the Robin Hood. Boddingtons decided to keep the Red King on the basis that it was larger, newer and a better situated premises. It was also fully licensed. The Robin Hood on the other hand was only licensed to sell beer, it was a much older building and also a lot smaller.

Louie Schofield recalls

'When we were first told that the pub was to be closed down, my mother was heartbroken. Father seemed to accept it, but Mother was inconsolable. I was nearly fifteen by then. It was a very sad time. We appealed against the closure and all the customers supported us, but it was all to no avail.

*Photograph B: Clarence and Bertha Briggs, the last tenants of the Robin Hood seeh here on holiday in 1952*

*Photograph C: Louie Schofield with a brandy glass etched with 'Robin Hood'(Photographed 1991)*

*Photograph D: Between 1916 and 1918 Geo Frederick Hamnet was landlord. His name can be seen over the door*

Page 85

*A History of Whitefield Pubs*

**Photograph E: William Blakely's name is over the door on this picture. He was tenant from March 1918 to July 1921**

We closed as a pub for the very last time on 31st December 1935. We continued to live in it as a house until June 1936 when we moved into a new house in Charles Street.

Louie still has one of the Tap Room stools in her kitchen and in her display cabinet a brandy glass etched with Robin Hood. When I asked Louie why the pub had brandy glasses when it was never fully licensed, she just poured herself a brandy and gave me a mischievous wink! God bless you Louie.

A list of all known licensees follows

Martha Hill later bought the Albert on Ribble Drive (then Oak Lane). Robert Fitton moved along the lane to the Travellers Inn.

Mr Nelson Burdaky who was later killed outside the Coach and Horses when he was run over by a lorry in 1928 can be seen on photograph D, third from the right outside the Robin Hood which was one of his favourite pubs.

Below is a restored version of this badly damaged photograph showing the missing section of the Bar Parlour window and the gentleman's (extreme right) missing foot. The crease across Mr Burdaky's left shoulder has also been eliminated.

Mrs May Barker who loaned this photograph is Mr Burdaky's granddaughter (see Coach and Horses pp 34-38).

The following was once printed on a card which was displayed in the window for many years:

*'Kind gentlemen and yeomen good come in and sup with Robin Hood. If Robin be begone come in and sup with Little John!'*

### Known Licensees

| Name | Date |
|---|---|
| Nathan Crompton | 1850s - 1860s |
| Ellis Hill | 23 2 1874 |
| Alice Hill | 26 5 1877 |
| Martha Hill | 21 5 1883 |
| Mark Hill | 18 4 1904 |
| James Leach | 19 9 1904 |
| Robert Fitton | 7 2 1907 |
| William T Humphreys | 6 9 1915 |
| Geo Frederick Hamnet | 17 7 1916 |
| William Blakely | 14 3 1918 |
| Robert Farrand | 11 7 1921 |
| Clarence Briggs | 21 10 1926 |

*A History of Whitefield Pubs*

# Red King (and William IV)     Bury New Road

*Photograph A: The Red King circa 1915, approximately 30 years old. Note the additional door into what was the vault, now altered to form part of the bay window.*

The origins of pub names are varied and many ranging from trades and professions, sports and pastimes, natural history, military achievements, heraldry, national and local heroes to local folklore. However, on this occasion we enter the realms of fantasy. The 'Red King' is a character in 'Alice through the Looking Glass' by Lewis Carroll in 1872. His Queen was intended by Carroll to be the concentrated essence of all governesses.

An unusual origin to reflect on. However, the pub does have a real history. The Red King public house was built in 1885 as a replacement for the William IV, a beerhouse which had stood approximately where the lamp standard is at the entrance to Moss Lane, as seen on photograph A which was taken around 1915.

William IV was born in 1765 and died in 1837. He was the third son of George III and succeeded his brother George IV in 1830. The year of his death, 1837, is the year the William IV beerhouse opened and took his name. It had originally been a shop and dwelling but had been converted internally. It even had its own brewhouse for its own supply. In 1838 it was listed as one of Whitefield's nine public houses in local directories. A directory for 1843 lists a John Mills as the owner and by 1864 the registered owner is a Samuel Briggs and then Robert Briggs' executors.

The Rate register for 1864 lists the William IV as: public house,

*Photograph B: The 1970s. Notice the location of the 'Licensed to sell' board over a no longer existent door!*

Page 87

# A History of Whitefield Pubs

*Photograph C: The new extension - Sympathetic to the style and symmetry (photo 1990)*

kitchen, stable, brewhouse, stable and loft. Rateable value £45-13s.-9d.

In 1879 the Manchester to Bury Railway line was completed and by the early 1880s plans were being made for a Whitefield train station. It was decided to build the station at the end of Moss Lane which was little more than a narrow track in those days, and so the William IV, by now an ageing building, was pulled down. Much controversy was caused about the planned site for the station and eventually it was decided that the Cow Lane site (the present site, now Stanley Road) was more suitable. A deciding factor for scrapping plans for a Moss Lane Station was the fact that Parliament would not sanction a level crossing so close to a station. Eventually, the railway was in fact bridged at Moss Lane.

Moss Lane was rebuilt into a more modern thoroughfare giving much improved access from Bury New Road and everybody was happy. The town now had a new lane, a new pub and a new railway station.

John Hacking had jointly owned the William IV with a Mrs Ann Briggs who must obviously have been related to the earlier Briggs's. He was the registered owner of the new Red King.

> John Hacking built a two storey building at the rear and offered it to the Besses o'th' Barn Band as a practice room and possibly a social club, but he died shortly afterwards. The band convened a meeting for discussing the feasibility of the suggested adaptability of the building for a practice room and club. The meeting ended with a resolution being adopted, appointing and authorising a deputation consisting of three or four band members to approach the late Mr Hacking's relatives to discuss acquiring the premises.
>
> Discussions took place and ended satisfactorily and a special meeting of band members and honorary members was called for the purpose of adopting, or otherwise, Mr Hacking's terms which proved to be £10 per year rental, with the option of purchase at any time for £150.
>
> The band purchased the building and formed a company known as the Besses o'th' Barn Social Club and obtained a drinks licence. The club has been very successful and it has helped to keep the band on its feet over the years and exists to this day.

Boddingtons Brewery bought the Red King around 1900 and have retained possession ever since.

There are a number of inscriptions carved into the stonework on the outside of the Red King. On the wall along Moss Lane, one reads *'There is a measure in everything'*. Higher up on the same side there is an ornate inscription. It is hard to make out, but it could be the initials 'RB', which are the initials of the original owner, Robert Briggs. Over the front door it reads *'Welcome the coming, speed the parting guest'*.

Internally, of recent times, this pub has been robbed of its old Victorian charm by the removal of its walls, although the extension that was built on recently must be described as sympathetic to the symmetry and aesthetically pleasing to the eye.

### Known Licensees

| | | |
|---|---|---|
| John Hacking | | 1885 |
| William Thomas Grumby | 8 7 | 1886 |
| John Bell | 4 11 | 1901 |
| Nancy Jane Bell | 26 7 | 1906 |
| Walter Scholes | 19 9 | 1906 |
| Charles Edward Fish | 24 10 | 1907 |
| John Beeson | 27 12 | 1909 |
| Bernard M Mortimer | 15 10 | 1934 |
| Nellie Mortimer | 7 2 | 1935 |
| James Pythian | 13 4 | 1953 |
| Raymond Barraclough | 2 12 | 1954 |
| Annie Riley | 21 10 | 1959 |
| Doris Ellement | 26 10 | 1961 |
| Norman Pomfret | 8 6 | 1977 |
| Barrie J Davies | 6 9 | 1983 |
| Thomas Farrand | 19 7 | 1989 |
| Stan Story | 12 9 | 1990 |
| Denise Siner | 5 12 | 1990 |
| Thomas McDonald | 4 12 | 1991 |

# Rose and Crown      Bury Old Road

The marriage of Henry VII to Elizabeth, daughter of Edward IV, brought about the sign 'Rose & Crown', which symbolized the end of the War of the Roses between the houses of Lancaster and York.

Whitefield's Rose & Crown stood on the corner of Clegg Street and Bury Old Road (late Manchester Old Road) at Besses Junction, one corner of a triangle of pubs which included the Travellers Inn and the Junction Hotel. The site of the Travellers is now a piece of road (see Travellers text), the site of the Rose & Crown a grass verge. Only the Junction survived from the triangle (though not in its original form).

The Rose & Crown is now beyond living memory of even the oldest inhabitant of the town, and only a few reading this will have heard of its existence at all, and yet, in its day, it was part of the hub of the community. Very little is known about the pub, unfortunately; only a few licensees are known. The following text attempts, briefly, to 'bring back' the Rose & Crown, if only in our minds and imaginations. This at least will ensure its survival as a part of Whitefield's colourful pub history.

The drawing of the Rose & Crown above also shows the old terraced houses down the left hand side of Clegg Street. Nowadays only the ten houses on the right hand side are still standing. Opposite, on the corner of Higher Lane, stands the Travellers Inn, and opposite that, the old Junction Hotel.

The Beehive and the Besses Hotel are within a cock-stride of these three and if we also consider the other five pubs just around the corner along Higher Lane, it's not surprising that the Besses Junction area with its ten pubs suffered heavily through over-moralistic magistrates who used the 1904 Compensation Act to '*rid the town*' (their words) of this high concentration of hostelries.

*Artists's impression of the Rose and Crown in its heyday*

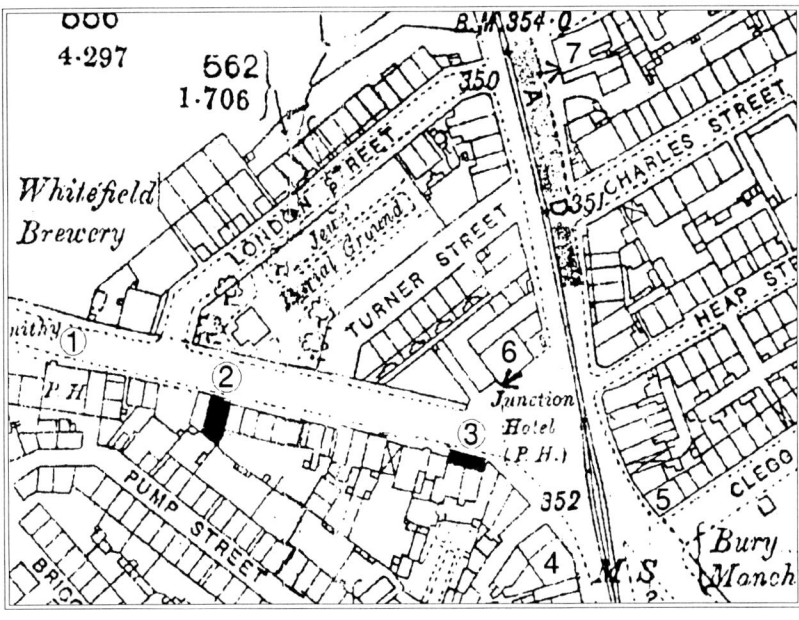

*Besses Junction 1893 showing (1) Bay Horse, (2) Foresters, (3) Robin Hood, (4) Travellers Inn, (5) Rose and Crown, (6) Junction Hotel, (7) Beehive*

> One of the few known licensees, Bob Francis' tenure at the Rose & Crown didn't run smoothly. On the 7th July 1873 he was found to have the pub open for business during un-permitted hours and was prosecuted. He appeared at the Bury Court on 13th July and was fined 20 shillings (£1) plus costs, and had his licence endorsed.
>
> He was in trouble again in 1876. On 9th September he was charged with permitting drunkenness on his premises and appeared back in court on 18th September. He was fined 20 shillings plus costs again, but this time he forfeited his licence and the pub was forced to close. The owner of the premises, Richard Turner, who lived in Walmersley Road, Bury, appealed against the closure and the licence was replaced at the annual Brewster Sessions on 3rd September 1877.

When Bob left the Rose & Crown, he moved into number 5, Clegg

## A History of Whitefield Pubs

Street; from here he ran a small coal merchant's business. Bob would loan small trucks for customers to take their coal home which he got from Outwood pit. He was known to keep people's change until they returned his trucks!

> In the 1860s and 70s, one of the regulars at the Rose & Crown in those distant days was a man who was known as 'Bobby Shortlegs' (real name Robert Whitworth). He had a normal well-built body of a six-foot man, but his legs were no longer than those of a young boy.
>
> It was quite common in those days for recruiting sergeants to visit drinking establishments. The usual ploy was to buy a likely candidate a few ales and persuade him to accept the 'King's Shilling'; quite often, they were tricked into accepting it.
>
> One night Bobby Shortlegs was sat in his usual place behind a table, which was hiding his legs, when in walked such a recruiting sergeant. Seeing Bobby's well-built frame, he offered Bobby the usual shilling. This and another were spent on beer, after which Bobby was asked to leave with the sergeant, who, apparently, was not amused as Bobby slipped off his stool, amidst a room full of laughter, and came round to join him. Needless to say, the sergeant left hurriedly without his recruit.

*Photograph A: A steam tram passing through Besses Junction*

*Photograph B: Taken in the 1960s from a similar position to photograph A*

*Photograph C: Compare with photographs A and B above. This one was taken from the same place in 1993*

The adjoining shop to the left of the Rose & Crown on the drawing on the previous page can actually be seen on photograph A. The pub itself was just right of the doorway, extreme right of this photograph. To the extreme left, the side of the Junction Hotel with its roofboards can be seen. The other building protruding to the right of the Junction Hotel can be seen much more clearly on photographs in the Junction Hotel text (pages 67-71). The steam tram dates this photograph between 1883 and 1904, after which the electric trams arrived. Photograph B, taken in 1963, shows Findlay's grocers in what was the Rose & Crown public house, and the adjoining shop, by now a greengrocer's. The new Junction Inn, just seven years old, showing its Dutton's sign, can also be clearly seen. Photograph C, taken in 1993, shows the site of the lost Rose & Crown as it looks today.

We do not know for sure when the Rose and Crown finally closed its doors as a pub. The scant evidence available points to a date around the turn of this century. It is the subject of ongoing research.

*A History of Whitefield Pubs*

# Seven Stars     Bury New Road

*The 'Stars' 1865 - 1909 to the right of the picture. The site is now a car park*

The Seven Stars was a favourite inn sign in the middle ages which still survives to this day (though not in the case of Whitefield's Seven Stars). It represented the seven starred celestial crown which the Virgin Mary was usually shown wearing. Sometimes it had an astrological meaning of significance, in which case the seven stars were represented on the sign board as a constellation.

Whitefield's Seven Stars Inn stood at 202 Manchester Road (now Bury New Road) on what is now the grassed area and car park in front of Whitefield Police Station. It can be seen on the photograph above (circa 1905) to the right of the Post Office at the end of the row of houses which still look exactly the same as they did then. It came into being around 1864/1865 as a beerhouse and was owned by Simeon Farrar who lived at Chapelfield (an area towards the Radcliffe end of Higher Lane).

The first tenant was Henry Holt who got himself into trouble for permitting gaming in the pub. On 15th August 1874 he appeared at Bury before Richard Bealey and Colonel Hutchinson, the Magistrates, on 24th August 1874. He was fined 40 shillings, plus costs, a heavy fine in those days. He died in 1879 and his wife Sophia took over the running of the pub until 1881 when finding it difficult on her own gave it up. In the same year the 'Stars' as it was affectionately known became the property of the Earl of Derby Estate who in turn leased it to the Whitefield Brewery Company. Around 1885 the Stars was granted a full licence.

In 1905 JW Lees (Brewers) Ltd of Middleton Junction became the new owners and shortly afterwards the 'Stars' became another victim of the 1904 Compensation Act when, in 1908 it was referred for compensation and ultimately closed.

The licence expired on 6th March 1909. For the next 56 years the building was used as a private dwelling house until 1965 when it was demolished. Shortly afterwards the new Whitefield Police Station was built just to the rear of the 'Stars' site (the original Police Station had been on Elms Street close to the corner of Bury New Road. This site is now part of Safeway's Supermarket car park).

An unusual feature of the Seven Stars was the downstairs front window sills. They were level with the pavement. Unfortunately the photograph shown is not very clear, or close, but is the only one the writer has been able to locate after many years of searching. Despite this, the sign board (though not legible) above the front door can just be seen, given careful scrutiny.

### Known Licensees

| | |
|---|---|
| Henry Holt | 1860s |
| Sophia Holt | 23 10 1879 |
| John Ramsbottom | 24 3 1881 |
| Frederick Duram | 8 7 1886 |
| James Mann | 23 5 1889 |
| John Frederick Carter | 15 1 1891 |
| William Lawson | 28 8 1892 |
| William Boyle | 27 5 1897 |
| Joseph Wood | 21 5 1900 |
| David Heywood | 16 9 1900 |
| Samuel Nuttall | 14 2 1901 |
| Thomas Holden | 22 8 1901 |
| John Taylor | 14 7 1902 |
| James Blant | 11 2 1904 |
| Josiah Wedgewood | 26 7 1906 |
| Chris Rothwell | 25 3 1907 |
| Nathan Hampson | 23 12 1907 |

# Travellers Inn  Bury New Road/Higher Lane

*Photograph A: Taken in 1887, Queen Victoria's Golden Jubilee Year (flags hang from windows)*

The Travellers Inn was located at 49 Bury New Road on the corner of Higher Lane and opposite the Junction Hotel. Nowadays the left hand 'filter lane' into Higher Lane at the junction traffic lights passes over the actual pub site. Recently a McDonalds drive-in and Aldi Supermarket have been erected within yards of where the old inn once stood.

In the early days the beer was supplied by the Whitefield Brewery which was only 150 yards away. An old rate book tells us that in 1864 these premises complete with stables were rated at £15-6s.-0d. James Jones was the landlord in 1870. He got himself in trouble for selling ale at 7.30am on a Sunday morning and at the hearing in Bury on 25th July 1870 he was fined 20 shillings plus costs. He must have learned his lesson as he ran the pub (and stayed out of court) for another eleven years and retired on 13th January 1881.

Issac Jackson took over from him and a census return for that year describes Issac as a Beer seller, aged 53 along with his wife, Mary Ann Jackson, housekeeper, aged 45 and Sarah Jackson, daughter, cotton weaver, aged 24. Issac died early in 1886 and the Licensing Records show that on the 8th July 1886 Mary, his wife, took over.

The photograph above, the only known one in existence for this period, was taken in 1887 during Queen Victoria's Jubilee celebrations. The photographer was William H Martin of The Studio, Prestwich. The lady in front of the doorway and wearing a white blouse is Mary Ann Jackson, the landlady. Mary's daughter, Sarah, is on the extreme right of the group (left hand across her waist). The stoutish man wearing a bowler hat and dark overcoat (slightly right and front of the picture) is Mr Wright Blackley, the landlady's brother and uncle to Sarah. Next to him (right and behind) and wearing a straw boater hat is Mr Thomas Wardle the tailor whose shop was at Number. 1 in the next block (extreme right of the picture). He also held the licence at the Bull's Head.

Next to Mr Wardle and wearing a cut-away frock-coat and flat cap is Mr Alfred Eckersall the clogger. He's standing outside his own shop which adjoined the pub. His name can be seen on the sign to the right of the Travellers Inn sign; under his name the rest of the sign reads 'Clogg, Boot and Shoe, Warehouseman'. As a point of interest, Alfred Eckersall's son was once Whitefield's only postman and the second cottage in the next block, Number 3, was the Whitefield Post Office. Out of the picture but three doors further right stood the Robin Hood.

Mary Ann Jackson died on 19th October 1897 aged 61 and was interred at Stand Chapel on 22nd October 1897. It is a sad reflection of those times to note that Mary could not write even her own name, nevertheless she made her mark - a simple cross - on her Will leaving £360-15s.-11d, a small fortune in those days. It is not known for certain how many friends and relatives attended the funeral, but it is known that the grocer's bill for the refreshments came to a little over 30 shillings (£1.50); today, the tea cakes alone would cost much more.

The next licensee was Robert Marsh and he officially took charge on 16th December 1897. Up to this stage the pub had only had two owners, the first being John F Fletcher and then the Earl of Derby Estate, which it seems acquired the deeds sometime around 1886, shortly after which the Travellers became part of the Whitefield Brewery property estate which eventually was absorbed by JW Lees (Brewers) Ltd of Middleton Junction. Four more licensees followed Robert Marsh and they were William Hampson July 1910, James Boardman Howarth December 1914 and James Hilton February 1926. On 5th July 1930 Robert Fitton, who was a very well known wrestler and local publican took over. He had kept the Robin Hood a few doors away from 1907 - 1915. He had also held the licences at the Albion in Prestwich Village (the Midland Bank [now closed] stands on the site), and at the Wheatsheaf.

The Travellers Inn was de-licensed and closed its doors as a pub on 31st December 1935. Shortly afterwards the front of the building had a face lift and was tiled and re-opened as Bennett's Butchers. It remained as such until the 1960s when it was demolished for road widening works. At the time of demolition, Alfred Eckersall's clog shop which had adjoined the pub had become C Brumby's and what was the tailor shop of Thomas Wardle by 1925 had become Yates' Hardware shop.

Mary Ann Jackson's daughter Sarah who was 30 when the picture was taken married a Mr Walter Carden and they had a son called Harry. He was only a toddler when his grandmother died on 19th October 1897. Up to that time he had lived at the inn with his parents. Harry was able to identify and name the people on the photograph for us. Harry in later years lived in Hardmans Road, but died some years ago when he was in his eighties. He was the last known link with the Travellers Inn.

This little corner of Whitefield bears no resemblance to what it used to. The buildings that now occupy this site have only a 'temporary toytown' appearance. Who will write of them in 100 years time.

| Bill for groceries | |
|---|---:|
| 9lb Ham | 6s-0d |
| 1lb Tea | 1s -6d |
| 4lb Cheese | 3s -0d |
| 4 jars of pickles | 2s -2d |
| 4lb Currant Bread | 2s -0d |
| 2lb Seed Bread | 1s -0d |
| 16 Tea Cakes | 1s -2d |
| 6lb Best Butter | 7s -6d |
| Tub of Mustard | 5d |
| 12 2lb loaves | 3s -6d |
| 10lb Loaf Sugar | 2s -1d |
| Total | £1-10s 4d |

*Photograph B: Taken from outside the Junction Hotel circa 1918/19. The Travellers Inn is on the extreme left of the picture (see photo photograph A). Note the circular seat around the lamp post*

A History of Whitefield Pubs

# Wheatsheaf Hotel   Bury New Road

*Photograph A: Stand Unitarian Church Whitsuntide procession passing the Wheatsheaf Hotel circa 1920 when it was an Atlas Brewery house*

The Wheatsheaf has been a popular inn sign since the 17th century and appears in several Coats of Arms, including those of the Worshipful Company of Bakers (1486). It is also one of the devices on the Arms of the Brewer's Company (now Society).

We start this particular pub history at 1727; the following details are taken from the deeds which are held by Robinson's Brewery.

On 22nd February 1727 Jane Ogden of Whitefield, a widow leased the premises to Sam Ogden, her son, who was a shoemaker. The lease stated '*All these two bays of building in Whitefield, containing one dwelling house, one parlour, one buttery, one milk house and two chambers over them, and all that orchard near the said building*'. The next entry is an assignment dated 17th November 1783 from John Ogden (probably Sam's son) to the executors of John Wood, Samuel Bent (otherwise Wood) Lawrence Fogg and John Royle.

On 4th June 1786 John Ogden and others assigned the premises to James Walker. In 1823 an abstract of title declared the premises are still held by the 1727 lease. A Peter Walker is mentioned in the entry (is this James Walker's son?).

It is in this year of 1823 in an announcement that the premises are to be sold by public auction. It is also the first time that it is described as the Wheatsheaf. Mentioned also is the brewhouse and stable. Bidding started at £500 and a condition was made that bids should increase by sums of no less then £5.

It seems that Peter Walker acquired the Wheatsheaf at this auction but how much he bid is not recorded. On 6th June 1823 Peter Walker sold the Wheatsheaf to William Sergeant of Manchester, 'Gentleman' and Edwin William Sergeant of Manchester, 'Gentleman'. The next assignment is dated 12th November 1823 from EW Sergeant to Elizabeth Openshaw and Edward Partington who were in possession of the premises at £50 per year rent.

The next entry on the deeds is a covenant which states that George Mills who lived next door had '*The privilege to fetch and carry water at all times and seasons from the pump standing upon the premises except in the forenoon of such days as the occupier of the said Wheatsheaf public house shall be brewing malt liquor for the House consumption, he and they paying one half of the expense of repairing such pump*'. On 1st February 1832 Jonathan Openshaw, a cotton spinner of Bury, assigned the pub to James Mills, who was a provision dealer.

The Chief Constable's report of 1889 gives the Wheatsheaf address as 254 Bury New Road and states the inn had no spare beds for travellers but could provide food for up to 60 people and had stabling provision for 2 horses.

Page 94

The next entry in the deeds is dated 1895. It says the house next door was now occupied by a Jonathan Mills who was the son of James. The Wheatsheaf was sold to George Mills (another son of James?) whose address was given as the Bricklayers Arms, Cheetham Street, Rochdale, which implies that he was already in the licensed trade

It appears at this stage that for quite some time the premises had been occupied by a Mary Entwistle at a yearly rent of £60.

Probably the most significant entry in the deeds is the next one, as the pub left private ownership. On 12th November 1895 George Mills of Broom Vale, Bury New Road, sold the Wheatsheaf to James Kay of the Atlas Brewery for £2,775.

The Atlas Brewery was at 225 Stockport Road, Longsight. In 1896 James Kay merged with Beaumont & Heathcote of the Standard Brewery, Jenkinson Street, Chorlton on Medlock to form Kay's Atlas Brewery Ltd. The new company now had an estate of 125 licensed houses. Brewing was concentrated at the Atlas Brewery and the Standard Brewery was sold. The premises later became a chocolate factory.

In 1929 Kay's Atlas Brewery was taken over by Robinsons Brewery of Stockport and the brewery was closed down in 1936. Robinson's was originally founded in 1838 by William Robinson when he purchased the Unicorn Inn in Stockport. Brewing began at the Unicorn Brewery, Lower Hill-Gate, Stockport around 1865. It was not until 1876 that they began buying pubs and by 1890 only 12 licensed premises were tied to the brewery.

**BEAUMONT & HEATHCOTE,**

**MILD**

AND

**BITTER ALE & PORTER BREWERS,**

**JENKINSON-ST., OXFORD-ST., MANCHESTER.**

*1863 Advertisement*

***Photograph B:** Front pane of one of the superbly acid etched bay windows*

***Photograph C:** Side pane depicting a wheatsheaf*

*A History of Whitefield Pubs*

Robinson's trade mark, the Unicorn, is of great historical interest; it also features in the arms of the worshipful company of wax chandlers (1483) the worshipful company of goldsmiths (1327) and the worshipful society of apothecaries (1617). The horn was thought to possess magical properties and was believed to be an antidote for all poisons. Two Unicorns support the Royal Arms of Scotland. When James VI of Scotland became James I of England, one of these Unicorns displaced the Welsh Dragon on the English Royal Arms, the other supporter being the Lion. There are also many allusions to this legendary animal in the Old Testament.

A list of known licensees follows and it is interesting to note a large proportion of ladies have held the licence. The names in brackets refer to the Directory whence the name has been taken.

### Known Licensees

| | |
|---|---|
| Edward Partington* (Baines') | 1823 |
| John Sidebottom (Heap's) | 1843 |
| Mary Entwistle (Barret's) | 1883 |
| Alice Entwistle | 25 5 1889 |
| William Butterworth | 16 12 1897 |
| Robert Taylor | 24 7 1911 |
| Thomas Coyne | 21 7 1913 |
| Richard Cooper | 18 12 1913 |
| Thomas Shaw | 23 10 1922 |
| Robert Fitton | 27 7 1925 |
| William E Brickles | 5 6 1930 |
| Emma Brickles | 15 7 1940 |
| William Sinclair | 27 11 1947 |
| Trevor F Felix-Thomas | 18 8 1949 |
| Robert Barkess | 2 9 1954 |
| Stewart Rock Price | 2 2 1956 |
| Mildred Jane Cotter | 23 7 1956 |
| Mildred Jane Maguire | 28 5 1957 |
| Edward A Maguire | 27 5 1959 |
| Thomas J Scott | 3 9 1968 |
| Louise Hounslow | 17 5 1971 |
| Beryl Monaghan | 7 2 1972 |
| Joan Pursglove | 10 7 1984 |
| Marjorie Bailey | 3 2 1987 |
| Norman Burdaky† | 4 12 1991 |
| Wendy Healey | 27 7 1992 |

*Edward Partington is also listed in a directory for 1818
†Sadly Norman Burdaky's tenancy was very short. He died in 1992.

*Photograph D: The Wheatsheaf photographed in 1991*

*Photograph E: The original mosaic porch floor (Photo 1992)*

*Photograph F: Robinson's trademark, the Unicorn. It has many historical connections in coats of arms in this country*

One story that has survived the passage of time is about the traveller who, on a hot summer day, called at the Wheatsheaf and asked for a quart of ale.

As it was being served to him a local man bet him a penny that he could drink exactly half of it, not a drop more or less. The bet was accepted, upon which the Whitefield man drank the whole quart without allowing the mug to leave his lips. Replacing it back on the bar he remarked 'Aw do believe aw've lost me bet' and paid his penny to the unamused traveller, thus getting a very cheap quart of ale!

# Woodman Inn

## Bury New Road

Many pubs bore this name over the centuries, typifying the importance of the woodman, a well-respected occupation in the old days. He looked after the forest and the woods and even the small groves, felling trees and generally keeping a close eye on things. Throughout Britain to this day we still have the 'Jolly Woodman', 'Woodmans Arms' and 'Woodmans Rest' to name but a few. Sadly Whitefield's Woodman Inn has long gone, but like the origin of the name itself, it will not be forgotten.

An old Groves & Whitnall (now Greenalls) property index book lists the Woodman as a beerhouse and four cottages, 204 Manchester Road and Woodmans Terrace, Whitefield. It was held on a lease of 99 years commencing 24th June 1814. We know it was next door to the Seven Stars where Whitefield Police Station is now (the Seven Stars was No. 202) but at some period over the years it appears the properties along this stretch of road were renumbered.

On page 21 of the 1883 Barret's Directory, the Woodman Inn is listed as being number 192. The most likely reason for this would have been that Manchester Road (at this point) was renamed Bury New Road.

In the 1860s George Warburton was the owner and licensee but on 24th February 1873 he appointed James Mather as tenant and transferred the licence into his name. James is also listed in the Barret's Directory as a beerhouse keeper. In 1887 George Warburton sold out to James Bullough, who, sometime around 1890, sold out to Groves and Whitnall.

It became another victim of the 1904 Compensation Act and its licence expired on the 9th October 1907. Like its neighbour the Seven Stars which survived slightly longer, it became a private dwelling house and was demolished along with the 'Stars' in 1965 to make way for Whitefield's new Police Station.

Construction on the station started in the middle of 1967 and was completed in May 1968 at a cost of £56,000.

Unfortunately no proper photograph, painting or sketch of the Woodman Inn has come to light, despite years of searching and intensive enquiries. However, a distant glimpse of the inn is possible. It can be seen to the right of the Seven Stars on page 91.

The known licensees of the Woodman Inn were as follows.

### Known Licensees

| | |
|---|---|
| George Warburton | 1843 - 1860s |
| James Mather | 13 3 1872 |
| Joseph Nathan Hampson | 2 9 1895 |
| Nathan Hampson | 30 9 1887 |
| William Peatfield | 22 5 1899 |
| Jane Nilkes | 11 5 1903 |
| William Yates | 2 4 1906 |

The map extract of 1893 shows the inn's location in relation to Morley Street which is still with us to this day. The bowling green to the rear of the Woodman and Seven Stars belonged to neither of the two inns as had previously been suggested. It belonged to the Liberal Club which was at 11 Morley Street. They took over the building in their heyday in 1887 for use as the Liberal party club house. It was not so successful, however, as the limited company of the club dwindled away to nothing by the early 1940s. A sub-tenant and shareholder Mr WE Brown, who had a school of dancing there kept up the place and paid the dues so that upon its liquidation in 1954, Mr Brown acquired the premises against his own assets. It has since been used by a one-man upholstery business, a bookmaker and the Whitefield National Spiritual Church and nowadays is in use by the Jehovah's Witnesses.

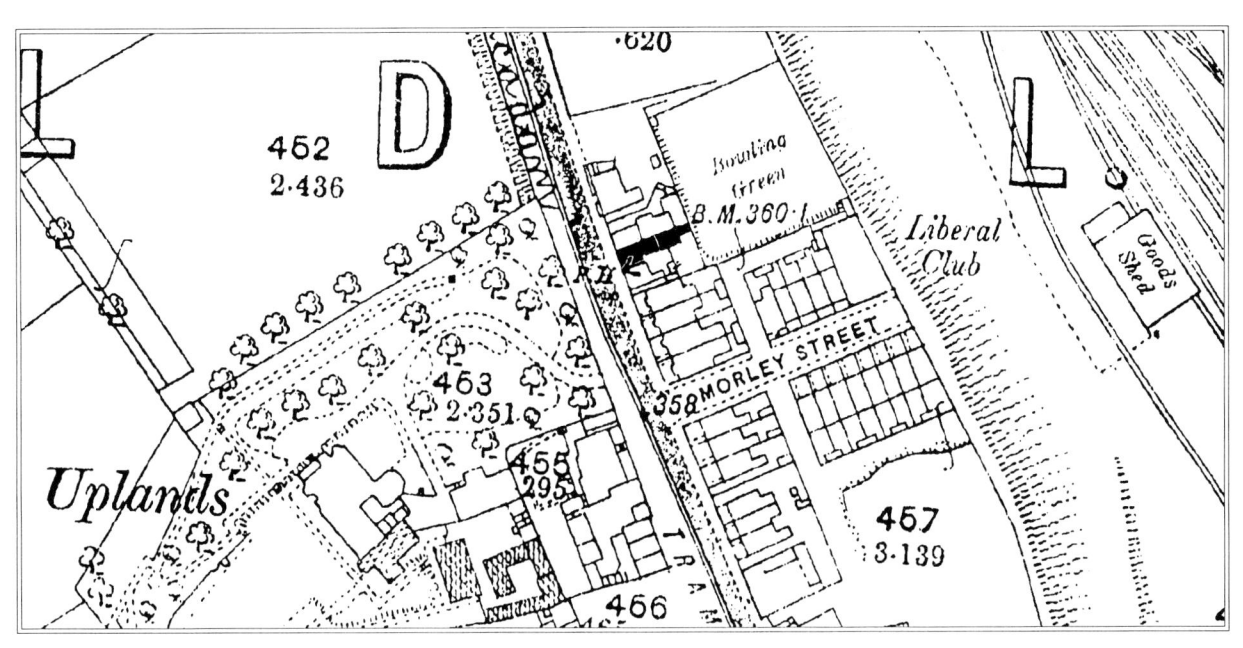

# Welcome Inn — Bury Old Road, Kirkhams

*Photograph A: The old Welcome with its unusual upstairs extension*

There are many Welcomes around Britain and they all signify hospitality. A few examples are the Welcome Return, Mossley, Welcome Traveller, Tyldesley, Welcome Inn, Accrington. Further afield examples are Welcome All, Stone Nr. Dartford, Welcome Hand, Rainham, Essex, Welcome Home, Newport, Gwent, Welcome Sailor, Fullbridge, Essex, Welcome Tavern, Belper, Derbyshire and another Welcome Inn, in Winchester.

Our own Welcome Inn was built in the early nineteenth century on part of a piece of land known as Rye Field. The earliest record of it being licensed comes from the 1850s when a shop and beerhouse was occupied by John Blackley, and later by Charles Howcroft, the Welcome became a tied house around 1890, when it was owned by a Tottington, Bury brewer by the name of William Greenhalgh. In return for a payment of £750 the licensee, James Catterall, agreed to sell only Greenhalgh's beer or pay £1 per barrel for all mild beer, strong beer and extra strong beer purchased from any other brewer.

When Edward Holt bought the Welcome in 1893, he paid William Greenhalgh £700 to release the Tie. A section of the contract to purchase the Welcome reads as follows: *'Land on the southerly side of Bury Old Road, Prestwich, containing 3,540 superficial square yards or thereabouts, with a frontage of 27 yards 28 inches, together with the beerhouse known as the Welcome Inn erected thereon'.*

> The Welcome, like the Coach and Horses has been included in this publication because of its proximity to the urban District boundary that divides Prestwich and Whitefield (it sits upon it) and because, like the Coach, it has always been frequented by Prestwich and Whitefield folk alike.

James Brooks became the landlord in 1921 and this was the year the Welcome was granted a full licence. A photograph exists of James Brooks in front of the Welcome; it is, however, too dark to reproduce successfully.

In 1925 Holts bought the lease on the land from the Earl of Derby Estate. In the same year Stanley Brooks took over the running of the pub from his father. Some of the older residents of the area recall that Stanley's son set up business as a coal merchant at the rear of the Welcome. People would take old bassinets (prams) to load up with coal. It seems he was a kind man for he would say to those who could not afford to pay *'Pay me when its warmer and thee'll not want a fire*.

> One funny story about the old Welcome Inn recalls a licensee who kept three silver campine birds in a pen at the rear of the pub. One day a stranger walked in carrying a sack and asked for a half pint of beer. Curiosity getting the better of the licensee, he asked what was in the sack. The stranger replied that it was a couple of silver campine birds he had for sale. 'I keep them' replied the licensee, 'how much do you want for them?' 'Thirty bob each' was the reply. 'I'll have them' said the licensee, 'and let me treat you to a pint as well'. 'Done', said the stranger. The transaction completed the licensee excused himself to put the birds with his others at the back of the pub. When he got to the pen, there was only one bird in it. He tipped the two birds from the sack into the pen and dashed back into the pub in disbelief. The pint he had poured for the stranger was still on the bar, but he had vanished. 'Done indeed', muttered the licensee to himself, 'I've been well and truly done'!

In 1935 building work on the present Welcome got underway at the right hand side of the old pub. The architect was N Hartley Hacking, whose office was at No. 5 Blackfriars, Manchester. Shown here is his impression of what the new Welcome would look like.

In April 1936 the new Welcome Inn opened and Stanley Brookes left the old pub to take on the new. Five months later a whist drive and dance was held in the large room upstairs to help boost the business in the new premises. Shown below is the front of the programme for the event; the original is stiff card measuring 3" x 5" and opens up like a small book. Inside are listed dances and space for 'engagements'.

*Architect's impression of new Welcome Inn*

Those were the days when you requested a lady to mark her card with your name if you wanted to dance with her. Shown also below is the dance list. The notice at the bottom of the programme says 'God save the King'.

A point of historical interest here is that technically we did not have a King at the time. George V died in January 1936. Edward VIII, his successor, was still uncrowned when he abdicated in December 1936. His coronation had been planned for 1937.

It is not known for certain when the old pub was knocked down, but until quite recently bits of the old foundations could be seen sticking up through the uneven land to the left of the pub, which is now used as a car park.

> Throughout the 1970s entertainment was provided by Ray, the resident organist, though I seem to recall it was forbidden to sing along to his music; also he had the organ positioned so that he sat with his back towards everyone!

At the time of writing, the Welcome has undergone its first refurbishment since 1936; the only other alteration that took place prior to this was the removal of the wall that separated the vault from the snug, effectively doing away with the snug

*The 1936 Programme*

# A History of Whitefield Pubs

to make the vault bigger. This work was carried out while Colin Openshaw was landlord.

Worthy of a mention whilst we are in the vault is the extra door next to the gents. This was the original Off-Sales door where many a jug of ale passed through, usually covered with a tea towel!

### Known Licensees

| | |
|---|---|
| John Blackley | 1840s-1850s |
| Charles Howcroft | 1860s |
| Robert Howarth | 1872 |
| Margaret Howarth (widow) | 1872 |
| E Howarth | 21 12 1883 |
| James Catterall | 1890s |
| James Dickinson | 1890s |
| (Widow) Dickinson | 1890s |
| Walter Redford | 17 10 1901 |
| (Widow) Redford | 1921 |
| James Brookes | 14 7 1921 |
| Stanley Brookes (Son) | 4 2 1925 |
| James A C Meakin | 9 2 1949 |
| William Hollingworth | 4 10 1949 |
| George E Slingsley | 3 6 1952 |
| Albert Livsey | 23 11 1965 |
| Colin W Openshaw | 2 12 1974 |
| Kevin Chris Smalley | 6 12 1991 |

All missing dates are being sought in ongoing research.

### Owners

William Taylor
John Blackley (Executors)
Charles Howcroft
William Greenhalgh
Joseph Holt Ltd

---

**RAY** has pleasure in inviting you to request your favourite tune and hand this slip to the waiter

PLEASE PLAY FOR ME

...........................................

and your name please

...........................................

*One of Ray's request slips*

*Photograph B: Coach trip to Southport in the 1930s*

*Photograph C: The Welcome Inn today (photograph 1991)*

*Photograph D: Welcome Inn sign*

Page 100

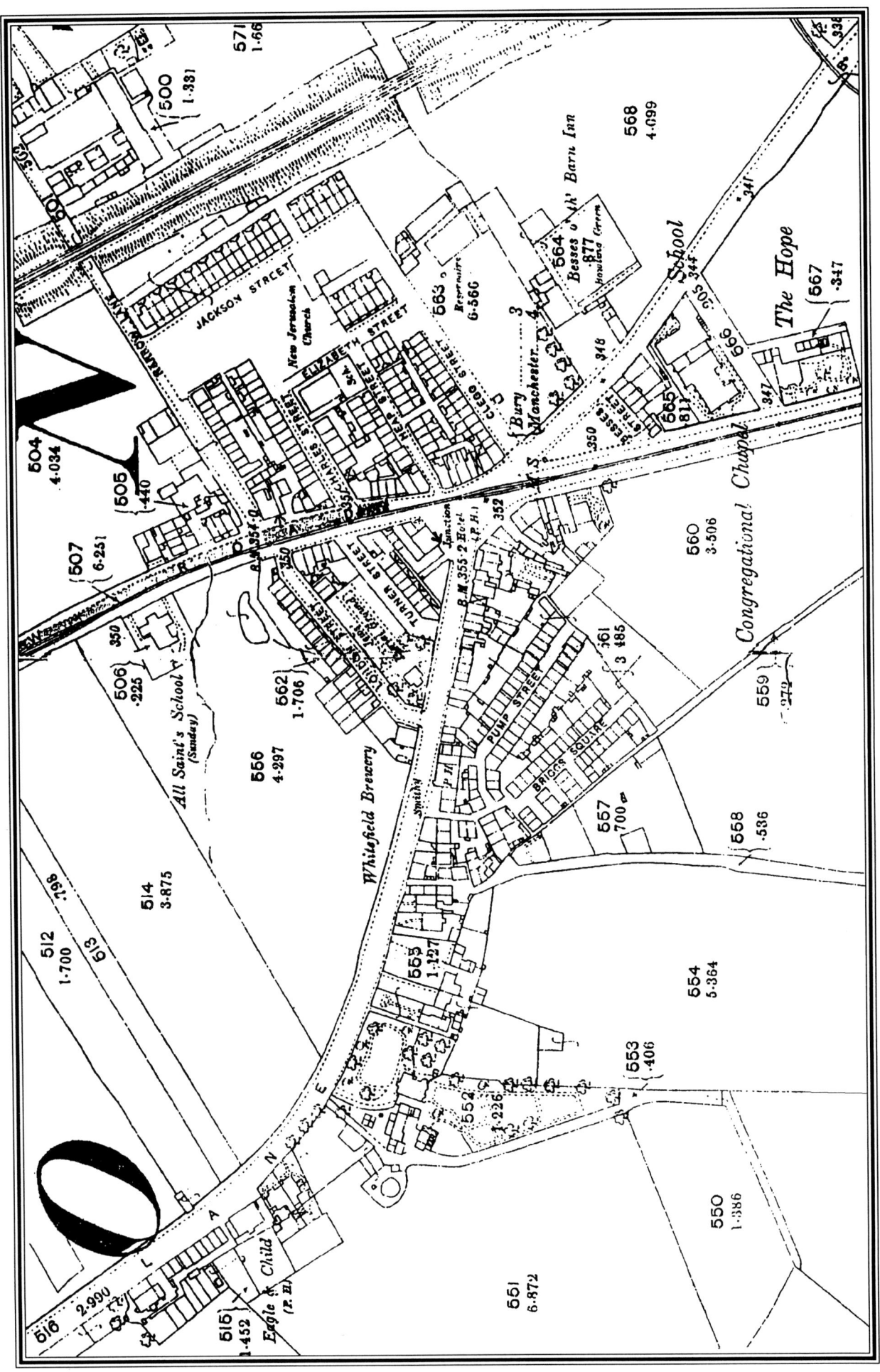

*1893 Ordnance Survey map showing the southern end of Whitefield*

# The Origin of Beer Engines

One seemingly insignificant but intriguing innovation in the public house, in fact one of the new technical devices of importance to come into it since the publican stopped brewing their own beer, was the Beer Engine. It was, from the first, a simple manually operated pump, incorporating no advances in hydraulic knowledge or engineering skill, similar in design to many pumps used at sea, yet perfectly adapted to its function in the public house.

It was brought into this environment by the need for speed and efficiency caused by the intensive demand in a busy city pub. Inevitably, most beer had to be stored in huge casks in the publican's cellars for the technical reason that it needed an even and fairly low temperature. This meant, equally inevitably, continuous journeying to and from cellars by the pot boys to full up jugs, a waste of time for the customer and of labour and trade for the publican.

Drawing up beer from the cellar at the pull of a handle at the bar at increased the speed of sale and cut the wage bill. Its invention has usually been deemed one of the minor accomplishments of Joseph Bramah, who patented the Hydraulic Press, a new lock and the improved water closet amongst many other devices. Certainly, he took out a patent for a beer pump on 31st October 1797 (Patent Office: Spec 2196), but it was not the device which came into commercial use. Only its purpose was identical. Drawings in the specifications show a man at ground level filling a jug with beer from a pipe

**Best Rubber Waste Preventor** for fixing to the spouts of engines, 4/- per doz.

**GASKELL & CHAMBERS, LTD.**
(Incorporated with YATES & GREENWAYS),
**BAR FITTERS.**
Manufacturers of Beer Engines and Hotel Bar Requisites, Counters, Back Fittings, Seating.
**DALE END WORKS, BIRMINGHAM.**

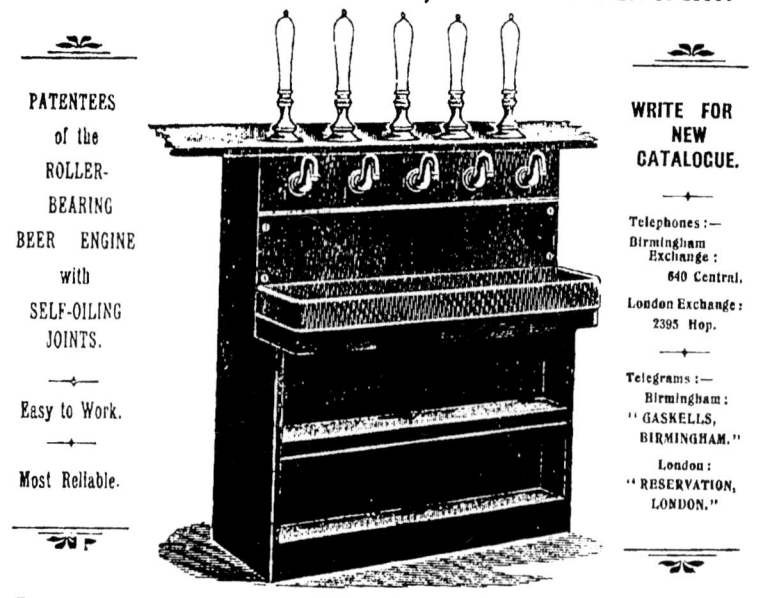

PATENTEES of the ROLLER-BEARING BEER ENGINE with SELF-OILING JOINTS.

Easy to Work.

Most Reliable.

WRITE FOR NEW CATALOGUE.

Telephones:—
Birmingham Exchange:
640 Central.
London Exchange:
2395 Hop.

Telegrams:—
Birmingham:
"GASKELLS, BIRMINGHAM."
London:
"RESERVATION, LONDON."

Patentees and Sole Makers of the "MERRITT," "DON," "SAFETY," and other Pattern
**CORK DRAWERS.**
**URNS AND MULLERS,** in MANDAL SILVER and other Metals.

**GASKELL & CHAMBERS (London) Ltd.,**
(Incorporated with SANDERS & SONS).
Works and Show Rooms—
**113, 114 & 115, BLACKFRIARS ROAD, LONDON, S.E.**

**Brass Pillar Counter Pump**
with ebony or porcelain handle and
Union, brass ... ... £2 15 0
Nickel plated. do. .. £3 12 6

*1870s Brass Pillar Counter Pump*

*1911 advert for 'Dalex' beer engines*

leading to storage vessels below ground. However, the pipe ends in a simple tap and the force which brought up the beer did not derive from a pump operated from above, but from a more complicated mechanism which would prevent the apparatus from being used in an ordinary public house. The innovator of the actual 'engine' which was to become universal in the next few years (who seems to have had no dealings with the Patent Office) remains unknown.

A 'Patent Beer Machine' was included with the fittings of a public house offered for sale in 1801. One of 'four motions' was sold in 1806 and two years later a similar apparatus appears in an accurate engraving. In 1812 at the valuation of equipment at the Crown, Crown Court, Fleet Street, one with 'three motions' could be described, *'with pewter sink, lead pipe, screw cocks and apparatus complete, fixed in a neat, inlaid mahogany case'* (the

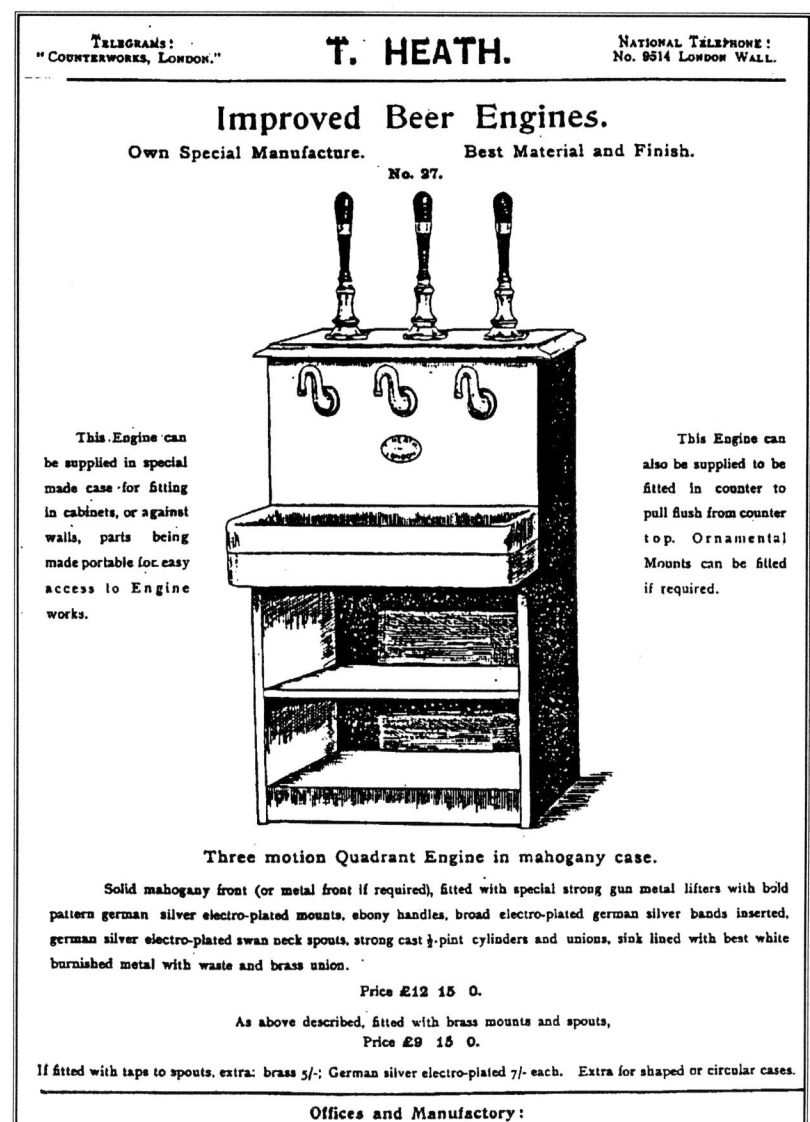

**Brass Pillar Counter Pump**
with ebony handle and union.
Brass ... ... £2 14 0
Nickel plated, do. £3 10 0

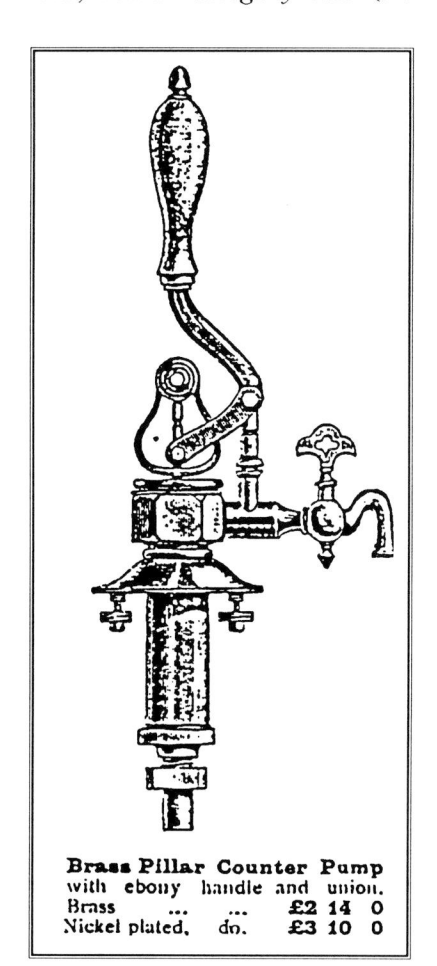

*1870s Brass Pillar Counter Pump*

TELEGRAMS: "COUNTERWORKS, LONDON." **T. HEATH.** NATIONAL TELEPHONE: No. 9514 LONDON WALL.

### Improved Beer Engines.
Own Special Manufacture.    Best Material and Finish.
No. 27.

This Engine can be supplied in special made case for fitting in cabinets, or against walls, parts being made portable for easy access to Engine works.

This Engine can also be supplied to be fitted in counter to pull flush from counter top. Ornamental Mounts can be fitted if required.

**Three motion Quadrant Engine in mahogany case.**

Solid mahogany front (or metal front if required), fitted with special strong gun metal lifters with bold pattern german silver electro-plated mounts, ebony handles, broad electro-plated german silver bands inserted, german silver electro-plated swan neck spouts, strong cast ½-pint cylinders and unions, sink lined with best white burnished metal with waste and brass union.

Price £12 15 0.

As above described, fitted with brass mounts and spouts,
Price £9 15 0.

If fitted with taps to spouts, extra: brass 5/-; German silver electro-plated 7/- each. Extra for shaped or circular cases.

Offices and Manufactory:
33, Rahere Street, Goswell Road, London, E.C.

*T Heath advert*

cabinet type beer engine as we know it today had arrived).

The first registered makers of beer engines were in London around the Blackfriars Road area. John Chadwell registered first as a 'Beer Machine Maker' in 1801. Thomas Rowntree also registered in 1801, then as a General Pump and Engine Maker of a 'double-acting beer machine' soon afterwards, if not from 1801. Within a few years there were dozens of manufacturers producing thousands of sets of beer engines to meet the demand for installations throughout the length and breadth of Britain.

By the turn of the century, handpumps on the bar were a common sight. By the 1920s and 30s there was hardly a pub in the country that did not have them. Ironically Bramah's patent was never operative, however, he did have better luck with his 'improved water closets' and after a few hours at the 'pumps' we can be grateful for that!

In T Heath advert above, the actual cylinders are not visible. That's because on these very early designs they were mounted in the cabinet and were generally directly below the handpull, similar to the bar-mounted type left and on the opposite page and therefore were concealed behind the fascia board which supported the spouts. Nowadays a new set of 'three pull' (as they are now known) beer engines built into a cabinet similar to the drawing above, would cost in the region of £800 - £1,000.

*A History of Whitefield Pubs*

# Epilogue

On the next few pages are a collection of facts, tales, poems and other beer or pub-related items. The illustrations shown on the pages are all related to breweries which have played some part or other in the history of the pubs of Whitefield.

## Interesting Facts

Beer has had a distinguished history in one form or another. For thousands of years Nomads of the Egyptian desert carried it around in cakes. Barley was buried in an earthenware jar until germination began then it was crushed and made into dough and baked until it formed a crust, carrying it this way was easier. Travellers merely had to soak it in oasis water until it fermented. The result was called 'Boozah'.

### Silver tongued

Few men have loved a pint of beer more than 18th century drinker Jedediah Buxton who believed that nothing quite matched the taste of a free one. Each pint bought him was logged in his notebook. By the time he reached the last page there were 5116. Each clearly as smooth as his patter.

*Ken Greenhalgh painting of a Crown Brewery drayman lowering wooden casks down a 'drop'*

### Drinking implements

In Saxon times horns and drinking cups were without feet so that the inclination was to drink them in a single draught. An early type of English drinking vessel was the 'Blackjack', which was made of a single piece of leather, the inside being treated with pitch for waterproofing and preservation. An old song goes:

'*A leather bottle is good, far better than glass or wood,
and when the bottle at length grows old, and will good liquor no longer hold,
out of its sides you may make a clout, to mend your shoes when they're worn out*'.

Pewter is very readily associated with drinking in inns and the ancient metal, a mixture of lead, tin and copper was well known to the Romans. About 1800 their popularity declined owing to their cost in relation to glass which was starting to be mass produced.

### Beer and the armed forces

Beer has long been a favourite drink with Britain's fighting forces. The record for the largest beer ration was held by the Beefeaters-Yeoman warders of the Tower of London until 1813. They each drew one gallon of beer a day to wash down their allowance of one pound of beef.

During World War II the NAAFI exported nearly four hundred million bottles of beer to allied forces all over the world.

At the height of a hectic battle in the Korean War, solders of the Black Watch regiment had to use their beer ration to cool their red hot mortars and when they ran out of ammunition, they threw empty beer bottles at the enemy.

### Beer and animals

In days gone by Danish pigs used to totter round their sties with a smile on their faces. It was connected with a farming practice of filling their troughs with strong beer to give the bacon a distinctive flavour.

A French lawyer named Bartholomew Chassenee made his reputation in 1521 by successfully defending rats which were accused of obstructing the flow of local beer by destroying a crop of brewer's barley. He argued that the summons should be served on all rats in the district and pleaded that the prosecutors cats were intimidating his clients by preventing them from appearing. He demanded a cash guarantee from the prosecution that the cats would not molest his clients on the way to court. As this, of course, was impossible the case was dropped.

### Königlich ......... what?

The longest word in the world of brewing comes from Germany.

Königlichbayerischeroberbiersteuerhaupteinkasserierer.

This was a title given to a Bavarian tax collector and translates as Royal Bavarian superior beer tax chief cashier. he was made redundant, along with the Bavarian monarchy.

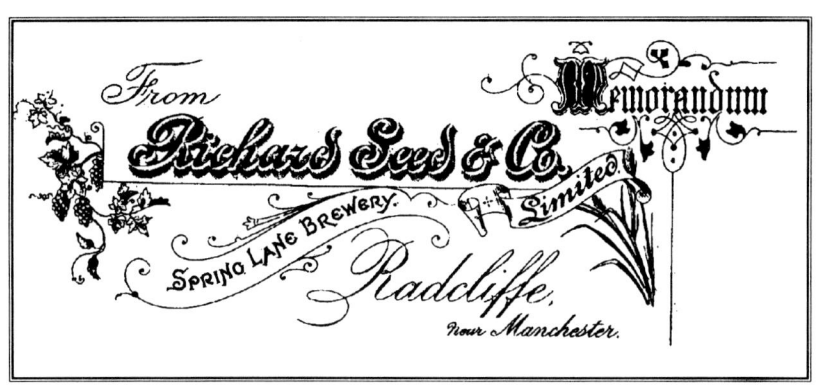

*A very ornate letter head from Richard Seed's Brewery in Radcliffe. The original was multicoloured and very attractive*

## A Celebration in Verse

Whoe're has travell'd life's dull round
Where'er his stages may have been
May sigh to think he still has found
The warmest welcome, at an inn

(William Shenstone 1714 - 1763)

The track o'life is dry enough
and crossed with many a rut
but, oh we'll find it longer still
when all the pubs is shut

Henry Lawson

### The Landlord Knows

He knows all our sorrows, he knows all our joys,
He knows all the girls who are chasing the boys,
He knows all our troubles, he knows all our strife,
He knows every man who steps out from his wife.
If the landlord told all that he knows,
He would turn all our friends into bitterest foes,
He would start out a story, which, gaining in force
Would cause all the wives to sue for divorce.
He would get all our homes mixed up in fights,
He would turn all our bright days into sorrowful nights.
In fact he would have all the town in a stew,
If he told one-tenth of all that he knew.
So when out on a part and from home you steal,
Drop in for a drink - the landlord won't squeal.

He that buys land buys many stones
He that buys flesh buys many bones
He that buys eggs buys many shells
He that buys good ale buys nowt else

Anon.

Poor John Stott lies buried here
Though once he was hale and stout
Death laid him on his bitter bier
In another world he hops about

Epitaph in an English Churchyard

## And a Few Tales

### Drunk and Disorderly

Asked why he was drunk at such an early hour, a Whitefield man informed the Bury Magistrates, 'I have just come out of a local clinic after having several weeks' treatment for my drink problem. I wasjust testing to see if the treatment had worked'.

### Time gentlemen Please!

Overheard in the Cross Keys some years ago. One sweet old lady to another *'I had my husband's ashes put inot an egg-timer. He was a lazy bugger when he was alive so he can damn well work now!'*

### 2p on beer!

After arranging a brewery trip around Samuel Smiths of Tadcaster, landlord Tony Bevington of Middlesborough's Cambridge Hotel was ashamed to find that two members of the party, having drunk a few too many free samples, proceeded to relieve themselves into a 1200 gallon tank of bitter. The brewery were not amused as they flushed away £7000 worth of ale

### Wet Excuse

The landlord of a Welsh pub who was prosecuted for watering down his beer, told the Magistrates that 'while hosepiping the cellar floor, water somehow managed to get through the spile hole of an open-vented cask'.

*Dutton's Brewery letterhead. The Dutton's logo was in blue*

## Some signs displayed in pubs in the town over the years

Free to sit and free to think,
Free to pay for what you drink,
Free to stop an hour or so,
When uneasy, free to go.

Our beer is good, our measure just,
Forgive us please, we cannot trust,
We have trusted many to our sorrow,
So pay today and owe tomorrow.

We have been pleasing and displeasing the public ever since we started.
We have also been cussed and discussed, robbed, lied to, held up, hung up and knocked up.
The only reason we are staying in business is to see what the hell will happen next.
Life is just one damned thing after another.

Call frequently
Drink moderately
Pay honourably
Be good company
Part friendly
Go home quietly.

## Left at the Kings Head right at the Crown!

Stop and ask anyone the way and it is likely you will be given directions using local pubs as pointers.

Inns have been with us for centuries, so it is hardly surprising that they are the most familiar landmarks around. Their colourful signs keep travellers on the right track (or lure them off it for a pleasant hour).

Pub signs have another significance. They are not only a living picture book of British history but were particularly important in days gone by when the ordinary person could not read but could readily understand a picture.

## Landlord! Beerhouse! Pub!

In modern day terminology we tend to refer to whoever holds the licence on a public house (whose name is over the door) as 'landlord' whether he or she be a tenant or manager, whereas in actual fact a landlord would be the owner. Throughout this book the owners (or landlords) have, where known, been mentioned as such. Occasionally in various texts the term landlord will have been used, not necessarily meaning the owner, but simply the person 'in charge'. Also to most people an establishment that sells beer will be a pub which is basically the abbreviation for a fully licensed public house. Nowadays, locally there are no beerhouses, establishments that were licensed only to sell beer. However, this book mentions several and they have been mentioned as such. Occasionally and loosely, there may be the odd reference to a beerhouse as the pub.

## Quotes

*For a quart of ale is a dish for a King.* Shakespeare (The Winter's tale).

*Find me a bench and let me snore, till charged with ale and unconcerned, I'll think its noon at half past four.* Kenneth Slessor.

*A man who exposes himself when he is intoxicated has not the art of getting drunk.* Dr Samuel Johnson

**An early photgraph of Dutton's Blackburn brewery**